"John Charvet's *Liberalism* is lively, opinionated, full of examples. and always admirably clear. The route fr   ader from actual liberal societies   now what liberalism stands for a
— *Jonathan Segl*   *UK.*

"This is a lively and original   es a distinctive understanding of   od- ern social life and provides   exploration of the role played by liberal ideas in contemporary political controversies."
— *Cillian McBride, Queen's University Belfast, UK.*

LIBERALISM

Liberalism: The Basics is an engaging and accessible introduction to liberalism. The author provides a comprehensive overview of liberal practices, liberal values and critically analyses liberal theories, allowing for a richer understanding of liberalism as a whole.

The book is divided into three parts:

- Liberal practices: the rule of law, free speech, freedom of association and movement, economic freedom and sexual freedom.
- Liberal values: freedom, autonomy, equality and the universal values of political societies – the communal identity – and well-being of their members.
- Liberal theories: natural rights, utilitarianism, Kant's rationalism and the contemporary theories of John Rawls and the post-Rawlsians.

Presented in a clear and concise way, this book will be an ideal introduction for students and scholars of liberalism, political philosophy, political theory and political ideology.

John Charvet is an Emeritus Professor of Political Science at the London School of Economics, UK. He has also been a Visiting Professor at Johns Hopkins University, USA, and a Visiting Fellow of the Australian National University, Australia.

THE BASICS

For a full list of titles in this series, please visit www.routledge.com/The-Basics/book-series/B

LANGUAGE (SECOND EDITION)
R.L. TRASK

MEN AND MASCULINITIY
NIGEL EDLEY

MEDIEVAL LITERATURE
ANGELA JANE WEISL AND ANTHONY JOSEPH CUNDER

MODERNISM
LAURA WINKIEL

NARRATIVE
BRONWEN THOMAS

POETRY (THIRD EDITION)
JEFFREY WAINWRIGHT

THE QUR'AN (SECOND EDITION)
MASSIMO CAMPANINI

RESEARCH METHODS
NIGEL EDLEY

SEMIOTICS
DANIEL CHANDLER

SPECIAL EDUCATIONAL NEEDS AND DISABILITY (THIRD EDITION)
JANICE WEARMOUTH

SPORT MANAGEMENT
ROBERT WILSON AND MARK PIEKARZ

SPORTS COACHING
LAURA PURDY

TRANSLATION
JULIANE HOUSE

LIBERALISM
THE BASICS

JOHN CHARVET

Routledge
Taylor & Francis Group
LONDON AND NEW YORK

First published 2019
by Routledge
2 Park Square, Milton Park, Abingdon, Oxon OX14 4RN

and by Routledge
52 Vanderbilt Avenue, New York, NY 10017

Routledge is an imprint of the Taylor & Francis Group, an informa business

© 2019 John Charvet

The right of John Charvet to be identified as author of this work has been asserted by him in accordance with sections 77 and 78 of the Copyright, Designs and Patents Act 1988.

All rights reserved. No part of this book may be reprinted or reproduced or utilised in any form or by any electronic, mechanical, or other means, now known or hereafter invented, including photocopying and recording, or in any information storage or retrieval system, without permission in writing from the publishers.

Trademark notice: Product or corporate names may be trademarks or registered trademarks, and are used only for identification and explanation without intent to infringe.

British Library Cataloguing-in-Publication Data
A catalogue record for this book is available from the British Library

Library of Congress Cataloging-in-Publication Data
Names: Charvet, John, author.
Title: Liberalism : the basics / John Charvet.
Description: New York : Routledge, 2019. | Series: The Basics | Includes bibliographical references and index.
Identifiers: LCCN 2018036867| ISBN 9780815362913 (hardback) | ISBN 9780815362920 (paperback) | ISBN 9781351111034 (master ebook) | ISBN 9781351111027 (web pdf) | ISBN 9781351111010 (ePub) | ISBN 9781351111003 (mobipocket/kindle)
Subjects: LCSH: Liberalism.
Classification: LCC JC574 .C488 2019 | DDC 320.51—dc23
LC record available at https://lccn.loc.gov/2018036867

ISBN: 978-0-8153-6291-3 (hbk)
ISBN: 978-0-8153-6292-0 (pbk)
ISBN: 978-1-351-11103-4 (ebk)

Typeset in Bembo
by Swales & Willis Ltd, Exeter, Devon, UK

Printed and bound in Great Britain by
TJ International Ltd, Padstow, Cornwall

This little book is dedicated to all those who have contributed to bringing about and defending, through their words and deeds, a liberal and democratic way of life, as a precious thing not to be lightly discarded or thoughtlessly despised.

CONTENTS

Acknowledgements	xi
General introduction	xiii

PART I
Liberal practices — 1

1	The idea of a practice and the initial distinction between liberal and illiberal societies	3
2	The rule of law	7
3	Free speech	17
4	Freedom of association and movement	33
5	Economic freedom	41
6	Sexual freedom	55

PART II
Liberal values — 61

7	The idea and value of freedom	65
8	The equality of the participants	79

9   Community   109

10 Liberalism and human well-being   125

PART III
Liberal theories   **137**

11 Libertarian theories   143

12 Utilitarian theories of liberalism   153

13 Kant's idea of freedom as rational self-determination 165

14 Contemporary theories of liberalism   175

    References   203
    Index   209

ACKNOWLEDGEMENTS

I wish to thank the following people for their time and trouble in reading and trying to improve earlier drafts of this work: Tony Amatrudo, Anne Charvet, Christopher Cherry, Alan Haworth, David Martin Jones, Eliza Kaczynska-Nay, Lloyd Reinhardt and Fred Rosen. I owe a special thanks to Matt Matravers for the many enjoyable occasions on which we have discussed the ideas of this book at length as well as for his painstaking efforts to improve several of its drafts.

GENERAL INTRODUCTION

This book is intended to be an introduction to liberalism. I understand liberalism both as a set of practices regulating important spheres of human life that have actually been adopted in many modern political societies, and as a body of ideas about what is valuable in liberal practices and why members of political societies should adopt them. As an introduction, the book is intended to be accessible to readers who have no previous knowledge of the literature on liberalism or on political theory more generally. All that is presupposed is that the reader has some experience of what it is to be a member of a political society interacting with other members on the basis of authoritative laws. The authority of the laws derives in the first place from the constitution which designates who has the right to make and enforce them. Although at any point in time the constitution settles (more or less) the question of what the laws are, any member of the society can always ask herself whether some other set of laws would not be better than the present ones. For modern states liberal laws and constitutions are one option. This book is written not just, or even primarily, for the student of politics and political theory but for the reflective citizen who is concerned with this question and wants to know how we should live together as members of a political society.

The book is divided into three parts: the first discusses liberal practices, the second liberal values and the third liberal theories. This tripartite structure does not chart a temporal sequence. I am not suggesting that, historically, liberal practices arose in some societies and then people started reflecting on the values embedded in these practices, and finally developed theories to show why liberal practices and values are superior to other possible arrangements of society, such as communism or fascism or religious authoritarianism. The sequence is, in the first place, a pedagogical one. If you set out, as I am now doing, to identify what liberalism is, what values it commits its adherents to prioritize and why they think that this is the best way for human beings to live together as members of a political society, then it makes most sense to begin with some description of what living together under legal and moral rules of a liberal character actually involves or is supposed to involve. This is what I mean by liberal practices. For example, a standard liberal practice is that of religious toleration. In a liberal regime, people are free to hold and express whatever religious beliefs they choose and are also free to engage in public worship of God in accordance with their beliefs. The laws, consequently, penalize any individual or state official who prevents or tries to prevent others from enjoying these freedoms. Hence, the members of such a liberal society interact, or are supposed to interact, in the sphere of religious belief and conduct by respecting each other's freedom.

The tripartite structure, however, also has a justificatory logic. If your aim is to provide a theory of liberalism that explains why it is better for people to live together under liberal practices, the best way of fulfilling it would be to begin with an account of what these practices are, explain what values are embedded in them and then demonstrate that these are superior values to those involved in liberalism's competitors. This book is first and foremost pedagogical. Its aim is to explain what it is to be a liberal, the range of interpretations liberalism is open to and why people think that liberalism is a good thing. One should be able to read this book, therefore, in order to acquire this understanding of liberalism while starting off with illiberal intuitions and ending up with those intuitions confirmed. Nevertheless, since much of Parts II and III of the book is concerned with good and bad arguments for, and interpretations of, liberalism,

I do not hesitate to make clear my own judgements as to where the better case lies.

How do we distinguish liberal practices from non-liberal ones? Not everything that a liberal society does is a liberal practice. Liberal societies are independent political societies prior to their members' decision to adopt liberal practices. As such they have interests and do things that they have in common with non-liberal societies. They are collectivities concerned with the general well-being of their community. They exist as one state in a potentially hostile multi-state world and so necessarily have to worry about their national security. Thus, we need some idea of what we are looking for under the category "liberal practice" in order to be able to identify liberal societies in the first place. While it helps to have actual societies widely regarded as liberal ones in order to identify the liberal core – we should ask what is distinctive about the practices of these societies – nevertheless, we still have to formulate an idea of a liberal practice as the preliminary focus of the enquiry into liberalism. From the perspective of our reflective citizen making a proposal as to how the citizens should live together, it could have been the case that liberalism did not yet exist. Let us suppose that she invents the idea of a practice in which the citizens respect each other's freedom in a certain sphere of life such as religion and tries to persuade her fellow citizens to adopt this experiment. She calls this idea liberalism. We would, then, have to explore how this idea might be worked out, what limits, if any, should there be to this freedom? If something like this idea already exists, then we can study how it is working in those societies that have adopted it.

The idea of a liberal practice that I shall be following in this book is one in which the participants in the practice interact by respecting each other's freedom. I shall explore this idea as it regulates people's interactions in the major non-political spheres of human life – our beliefs and their expression, our associations and movements, our economic and sexual relations. This idea already picks out a central value through which liberalism is being identified – individual freedom. Liberalism attaches fundamental value to leaving individuals as free as possible to decide for themselves what to believe, where to live, who to associate with and how to conduct their economic and sexual relations. But there is another fundamental value for liberalism implicit in this idea – the equal status of the participants in the practice. By this I mean that they all have the same rights. Whatever right one person has to hold his religious beliefs and practise his religion must be accorded to everyone else. In other words, freedom and equality must be interpreted together to form the basis of a coherent practice. For instance, suppose some people believe that their religion requires them to persecute, expel or even kill non-believers. To accord freedom to these people to practise their religion in respect of these particular beliefs would result in denying religious freedom to everyone else (not to speak of the denial of life). Hence, allowing the persecutors this freedom could not form part of a coherent practice in which every participant enjoys an equal freedom. Their freedom to persecute must be denied.

My account of liberal practices in Part I will be infused with the values of freedom and equality. Since freedom and equality have to be interpreted together in order to construct a coherent liberal practice, it may seem that the discussion of liberal values will unavoidably permeate Part I and that, consequently, Part II will be redundant. My justification for separating the discussion of liberal practices from that of liberal values is that there exist different ideas of what constitutes freedom and of what the grounds for equality are, and these different ideas affect how one thinks the practice of an equal freedom should be organized. These differences are particularly noticeable in the economic sphere. Broadly, one can distinguish a libertarian form of liberalism from an egalitarian one. The former purports to begin with a right to liberty and to play down the claims of equality, while the latter asserts the primacy of a demanding notion of equality over the claims of liberty. Yet, both are versions of an equal freedom and hence count as forms of liberalism.

In discussing liberal practices in Part I, I will note these different interpretations of the liberal idea without attempting to resolve the differences. Part II will focus on the meaning and value of freedom and equality, in the first instance, as the central concepts and values of a liberal society. This discussion constitutes a sort of half-way house between the discussion of the practices and the evaluation of theories. The discussion faces both ways because the issues raised point backwards to the discussion of the practices in which the values are embedded, and forwards to the theories that attempt to show why this or that understanding of freedom and equality is to be preferred and why liberalism is better than alternative ways of organizing society. The advantage of having a distinct half-way house is that it enables us to reflect on important issues in the understanding of freedom and equality without getting entangled in the more concrete account of practices, on the one hand, or the more comprehensive abstract theories, on the other.

By insisting on the context of an independent political society in which the liberal values have to be understood, I point to the fact that a liberal society must attach major importance not only to freedom and equality but also to the values of community and well-being. The liberal practices cannot be understood in a way that undermines the communal identity without which there would be no society and so no practices. Neither would it make sense to adopt liberal practices if they led reliably to a general immiseration. Community and well-being are not specifically liberal values. They are values any independent political society must pursue whether it is a liberal society or not. But as they are fundamental values for a liberal society, the liberal values must be interpreted in relation to them also. Hence, we will need an understanding of them which makes the idea of a successful and prosperous liberal community a genuine possibility.

Part III is concerned with theories of liberalism. By a theory of liberalism, I mean a body of ideas claiming to show how the liberal idea should be understood and why embracing the liberal practices and the values embedded in them is the right or the best way for human beings to live together as members of the same political society. This part will cover the main theories that have been historically prominent in modern political theory and also some contemporary theories that have received much attention. I cannot discuss all these theories in much detail in order to keep within the limits of an introduction. My aim will be to identify the main strengths and weaknesses of each theory as a theory of liberal practices. I do not think that any existing theory is satisfactory in this respect, and I will attempt to show how they can be improved.

FURTHER READING

A classic history of European liberalism is Ruggiero (1927).
A different sort of history is Fawcett (2014), which focuses on particular liberal figures as illustrative of themes and issues.
Freeden (2015) is a very short introduction concentrating on overlapping themes.
Wall (2015) covers many different topics: historical, normative, concepts and challenges.

PART I

LIBERAL PRACTICES

THE IDEA OF A PRACTICE AND THE INITIAL DISTINCTION BETWEEN LIBERAL AND ILLIBERAL SOCIETIES

I shall be using the term "practice" in this book to mean an invention by human beings of a way of interacting whose elements depend on the agreement of the participants. Games such as football are examples of a practice. While there are, of course, physical features of the world including human beings that make the game possible, the rules that constitute the game, and hence the game itself, exist only insofar as some human beings agree to interact in accordance with them. Money is a human invention, and its use as a store of value and a medium of exchange constitutes a human practice in the same way. It can serve these functions only if human beings agree to attach that sort of value to certain things such as pieces of metal, bits of paper, cowrie shells and so on. Political constitutions such as the rule in the UK that a valid law requires the consent of both Houses of Parliament and the monarch are also examples of human practices. The facts in the world created by such practices are sometimes called social or institutional facts. They do not exist in the way the solar system exists. The facts about the solar system and such things exist independently of human beings and their beliefs. They are natural facts. Social or institutional facts exist only because of human beings' inventive social schemes. They are, nevertheless, facts about the world.

When I say that practices exist only through the agreement of the participants, I do not mean that they come about only as a result of something like a formal contract to establish the rules of interaction or the meanings to be accorded to certain things and relations. Generally, they emerge through much more informal and unstable processes and only acquire a fairly determinate and durable form over time. In such a development, formal agreements may have their place. But they are not necessary elements in a practice.

Liberal practices are practices in this sense. They are inventions of a collection of human beings who agree to interact on the basis of certain rules. These rules may exist solely as the idea of some philosopher as to the ideal set of rules for a society of human beings to adopt. But insofar as an actual society adopts or develops them over time as the basis of its members' interactions, they exist as social facts constituting a liberal society.

While the next few chapters are devoted to a description of them, we need an initial identification of what is supposed to be liberal about them. The liberal character of these practices is standardly identified in terms of individual freedom, as in free speech or freedom of expression, freedom of association, free movement, economic freedom, sexual freedom. Liberal societies are supposed to enjoy these freedoms while illiberal societies do not. But it is fairly obvious that the distinction between liberal and illiberal societies cannot consist in the former having unrestricted freedom in these spheres and the latter having absolutely no freedom at all. The distinction must be one of degree rather than being a matter of black and white. Consider free speech. Liberal societies restrict speech in some respects. For example, they all have libel and slander laws. They all deem it illegal to incite people to commit criminal acts. Speech that constitutes an invasion of privacy, or endangers public safety, order or national security may be restricted.

It is equally obvious that no society prohibits its members from expressing themselves altogether. What these considerations suggest is that there are some fundamental interests of persons in respect both of their character as separate individuals and as members of a political collectivity that justify restricting speech in any society whether liberal or illiberal, but that illiberal societies interpret fundamental interests justifying constraints on speech in a more extensive way than liberal societies. This is how I will proceed in the following chapters on the substantive liberal practices. I shall begin with the standard constraints on individual freedom in each sphere to be found in liberal societies, and then establish the points at which illiberal and liberal societies part company with regard to what they restrict. However, in the case of the first chapter on the rule of law, the procedure will be slightly different. This is because the rule of law is essentially about the constraint on the exercise of arbitrary power by one individual over others and thus exists to protect to some degree the liberty of the subject. By requiring people in their interactions to follow rules, the laws enable individuals to pursue their interests without fear of arbitrary invasions by others. So, from the perspective of the rule of law, all law promotes individual liberty to some degree.

The above remarks indicate that the liberal or illiberal character of a society is a matter of degree. The degree can be charted over three dimensions: the number of people who enjoy the liberal freedoms; the number of spheres of life covered by them; and the extent of freedom in each sphere. Thus, with regard to the first, some categories of people may be excluded from liberal rights, such as women in all early liberal societies and racial or ethnic groups in some others (e.g. the United States, Australia, South Africa). The standard justification given for such exclusions is the incapacity of the members of the category to benefit from the freedoms by running their own lives. They are regarded as essentially dependent personalities who need to be governed by others. With regard to the second dimension, some societies may establish a high degree of economic freedom but have strict limits on free speech and association (contemporary China enjoys a considerable degree of economic freedom but very little freedom of speech). Others may have little freedom in any sphere except the sexual, and yet others much freedom in every sphere except the sexual. As for the third dimension, the extent of freedom in any sphere may vary from society to society. Thus, in many contemporary western societies, so-called hate speech is a criminal offence (e.g. the UK, France, Germany, Denmark, Canada and many others) as is holocaust denial (the denial that Nazi Germany murdered approximately 6 million Jews is illegal in most European countries and Israel but not the UK). But such constraints on free speech are largely absent in the United States. Even more obviously the extent of individuals' economic freedom may be anything from practically non-existent in North Korea to very high in Singapore.

I have been talking about freedom and constraint as they apply to the laws of a society. But another distinction is that between the coercion that is exercised through the laws and what John Stuart Mill called the moral coercion of public opinion. In his famous liberal essay "On Liberty" (2015; first published 1859) Mill was particularly concerned with the way in which public opinion could stifle freedoms that the law permitted by penalizing people, not through the courts but through social and economic ostracism. He sought to develop liberal principles that public opinion, and not just the laws, should follow. This issue is very much alive today in debates about political correctness and the denial of platforms to speakers deemed to have obnoxious views. I will discuss it in the chapter on free speech.

In the following chapters describing the liberal practices, I shall be concerned primarily with the idea of a fully liberal society – that is to say with a society that promotes and protects the greatest degree of individual freedom for all its members compatible with its viability and prosperity as an independent state. The reader should remember, however, that liberalism is a matter of degree, and that the adoption of some elements of paternalist, and hence illiberal, attitudes and policies in a society's arrangements does not mean necessarily that the end of civilization is nigh.

Liberal practices and ideas, especially in matters of religious belief and economic activity, first emerged in North Western Europe in the course of the 17th and 18th centuries, in particular in the economically dynamic states of the Netherlands and later England. The success of these practices in promoting peace and prosperity in these countries, and their effective transplantation to the United States, encouraged other European states to liberalize in the 19th and 20th centuries. This process of European liberalization was radically challenged, after the disasters and destruction of WWI, by the rise of the communist and fascist states. The defeat of the fascists in WWII and the collapse of the Soviet Union in the late 1980s led to an extraordinary outburst of liberal euphoria in which liberal thinkers came to believe that liberalism had now achieved a more or less permanent world-wide ideological hegemony. This belief rapidly turned out to be illusory, and the liberal-democracies once again face substantial challenges from authoritarian states of varying character, such as the managed democracies of Putin's Russia and his many followers, the scarcely believable communist capitalism of China and the medieval but oil-rich Islamic theocracies.

THE RULE OF LAW

The rule of law consists first and foremost in the development of constraints on the exercise of arbitrary power by one individual over others. Interactions between individuals, including and especially interactions between the more and the less powerful, must take place within the requirements of general rules laid down beforehand and accessible to all. A so-called rule which names particular individuals – such as one that says that John Smith is to be apprehended and executed – is not a general rule but a decree by a person on whose say so alone John Smith is to be done in. The rule of law bans such exercises of arbitrary power whether by private individuals or by state officials. In this sense, the rule of law is to be contrasted with the rule of men (or women). Individuals can only be apprehended by state officials or private citizens if they are reasonably suspected of violating a properly constituted law and must then be brought before a court and charged with the crime in accordance with fair procedures.

The great advantage of the rule of law is obviously enough that it gives protection to everyone for the enjoyment of the rights that are bestowed on her by the laws from invasion by more powerful persons. In this sense, individuals are enabled by the rule of law to do as they please within their rights. The rule of law necessarily protects whatever liberties the law accords them. You would think, then, that every regime, however illiberal, would aspire to promote and defend the rule of law in its domain. For the rule of law gives its members security and liberty (in the above sense) and would, thus, constitute necessary, if not sufficient, conditions for its members' prosperity.

One problem with this supposition is that the laws that the rule of law upholds may be very bad laws from the point of view of the interests of some of those subject to them. They may leave some people with very few rights and make them dependent to a shameful degree (from a liberal point of view) on the good will of their "lords". Thus, laws enforcing serfdom or patriarchy will not secure for the serf or for women the benefits I attributed to the rule of law – namely the security and liberty that enables a person to run her own life without being subject to the arbitrary will of another.[1] In this sense, the rule of law will not be of much benefit to people subject to it unless they possess a degree of property and liberty that gives them a certain independence. Thus, the rule of law will serve the feudal lord and the patriarch very well but not so well those over whom he rules. Nevertheless, having few rights and a large degree of dependence is better than having no rights and total dependence. So, the enforcement of the rule of law would give even the subjected some protection from oppression.

Another major problem is that the rule of law is directed at the restriction of the power of governments as much, if not more, than the power of private individuals. Indeed, governments have potentially vastly more power than private individuals, and this power could be, and often is, exercised arbitrarily to the detriment of their subjects. In the pre-modern age in which monarchical government predominated, monarchs tended to claim that their right to rule derived from God and that, as guardians of the law, they could not be subject to the law. Their sovereign legislative, executive and judicial power was necessarily an absolute power, so they could not be held to account for its exercise. Thus, while monarchs for the most part supported the rule of law for their subjects, they were not at all keen that their own exercise of power should be subject to law.

The story of the struggle in England to make governmental power accountable contains a number of well-known and acclaimed landmarks. In the first instance, there is the signing of the Magna Carta in 1215 by King John and a party of rebel barons. While this charter includes many provisions having to do with the substantive rights of the barons of little relevance today, one clause forbids the King to imprison anyone indefinitely without trial and another binds the King to follow due process in his courts and not to allow the justice provided to be for sale. Both these are fundamental principles of the rule of law. They may not have been closely adhered to by subsequent royal governments, but they remained as something to be appealed to by Englishmen concerned with their rights. Restriction of the power of the King to levy new taxes and imprison disaffected subjects through special courts, such as the infamous Court of Star Chamber, was a major issue in the English Civil War. The Stuart Kings (James I, Charles I 1603–49) used this court to suppress opposition to their policies. Its sessions were secret, allowed no appeal, and punishment was swift and severe. The court was abolished by act of Parliament in 1641. The victory of Parliament over Charles I in the 1640s, repeated over James II in 1685, led to the consolidation of these principles in a series of acts of Parliament. First, the Habeas Corpus Act of 1679: this required that a person arrested and imprisoned had, after a short period, to be presented in a court of law, charged with a crime and tried through due process. The Bill of Rights of 1689 forbade the monarch to interfere with due legal process. In particular, the monarch could not create new courts of law or act as a judge of law. Furthermore, the monarch could not levy new taxes without the consent of Parliament and could not maintain an army in peacetime without its consent. Other provisions further protected the rights of members of parliament against arbitrary executive power. The Act of Settlement of 1701, which settled the succession to the English crown in the German Protestant descendants of the Stuarts, also affirmed its significance for us – the principle of an independent judiciary. Judges were given a secure tenure, being removable only by parliament which at the same time undertook to follow a convention not to discuss particular judicial decisions.

Principles of this kind were adopted by the newly independent Americans in their Bill of Rights of 1789 and followed in the laws of the independent states of the British Commonwealth. They have been elaborated and affirmed in some sections of the UN sponsored

International Covenant on Civil and Political Rights, which came into force as part of international law in 1976 and has been ratified by a large majority of states. The relevant sections assert that no one shall be subjected to arbitrary arrest and imprisonment, that anyone arrested shall be informed of the charges against him, that he shall be brought promptly before a judge and entitled to a trial within a reasonable time or be released (article 9); that anyone brought to trial is entitled to a fair and public hearing by a competent, independent and impartial judge established by law and that he is to be presumed innocent until proved guilty, to have adequate time and facilities to prepare his defence and to communicate with legal counsel, to be tried in his presence and defend himself in person or through legal assistance, to examine witnesses against him and to obtain the presence of witnesses on his behalf, not to be compelled to testify against himself or to confess guilt (article 14); nobody shall be held guilty of any offence which did not constitute an offence at the time the act was committed nor suffer a heavier penalty than the one applicable at the time (article 15).[2]

All these are admirable principles of the rule of law, and with most states endorsing them you would have thought that the rule of law was being widely upheld in the contemporary world irrespective of whether a regime is politically liberal or illiberal. This is very far from being the case. There are two connected reasons for this. One is the inability or unwillingness of government leaders to prevent or drive out the widespread corruption of government officials in the legal system from police officers right up to judges. Justice is for sale to those with the deepest pockets. The other reason is the opposition of many government leaders to the application of the rule of law to government acts. They may reject such subjection of government to law outright or suborn the judges so as always to obtain the desired result because they themselves are deeply corrupt. Many are engaged in the theft of state property or funds for their personal account or to enable them to buy political support. Furthermore, with such leaders in place corruption is likely to permeate all levels of government.

Some of the worst abuses of the rule of law in the last 100 years have, however, been carried out by regimes that explicitly rejected liberal principles and the rule of law for an idea of the rule of the people's will. I have in mind the communist and fascist regimes of the 20th century. The communist regimes of Lenin, Stalin, Mao, Pol Pot and others justified themselves as leaders of the communist party that was supposed to be the embodiment of the people's will as workers, whereas the fascist leaders saw themselves as expressing the will of the nation. In both cases the leaders believed that their regimes' policies contained a superior justice based on the real interests of the workers or the nation that legitimated the lawless horrors they perpetrated on their own people. More recently, the successor regimes to these state terrorists in China and Russia have attempted to introduce some degree of liberal freedoms and the rule of law while maintaining the position of an authoritarian government above the law. The two cases are different. In China, the communist party still asserts its right to rule as the only interpreter of the interests of the workers while promoting capitalist development at a hectic pace and allowing its members to collude with the capitalists in acquiring control of state assets for their personal enrichment. Thus, while the regime sometimes talks as though it wants to establish an effective rule of law dispensing impartial justice, it knows that it cannot afford to do so. This is because of its members' own corrupt practices and because a rule of law that protected citizens' rights against an authoritarian government would allow opponents of the communist party monopoly to acquire a secure independence that would enable them ultimately to challenge communist party rule itself. It cannot, therefore, and will not permit an independent judiciary to be formed whose decisions it cannot control.

In Russia, by contrast, communist party rule collapsed before the process of privatizing state assets began. The result was a massive collusion between a few state officials and dubious entrepreneurs to sell off the assets at knockdown prices, thereby bringing into being an oligarchy of billionaires who have made their riches out of despoiling the state. The new Russia adopted a liberal and democratic constitution under the influence of western advisers. But the economic chaos and widespread impoverishment and insecurity that resulted from the attempted rapid transition from the extreme authoritarianism of the soviet regime to liberal capitalist forms led to the rise to power of Putin backed by the oligarchy. What Putin succeeded in doing was to preserve some of the forms of liberal democracy while ensuring that the centres of power were controlled by him and his cronies. He has effectively eliminated an independent press and television by the extension of ownership by the state and friendly oligarchs. He has cowed the judges into becoming complicit in his policies for dealing with opponents through trumped up charges and possibly outright assassinations. He has manipulated the voting system by the systematic harassment of rival leaders and parties through his control of the courts and probably by the use of fraudulent votes. In effect, he has succeeded in re-establishing an authoritarian government in Russia that does not hesitate to violate rule of law principles.

These considerations suggest that the core elements of a rule of law regime – the Habeas Corpus rule, an independent judiciary, the requirements of due process – are very unlikely to be achieved without the operation of other principles and institutions through which governments may be held to account for their actions. Thus, independent media supported by rules upholding free speech together with free association and movement would seem to be essential means for a people to become informed as to what its government is up to and to cooperate in opposing its policies. A non-corrupt democratic electoral system, on the other hand, can alone make it possible for the people to remove the government without the threat or exercise of violence. In that case, these liberal and democratic practices, while not strictly part of the meaning of the rule of law, are nevertheless essential elements in an effective system for holding governments to account and thus of making their actions subject to the rule of law.

If an independent judiciary is fundamental to the rule of law, it is also important that the judges limit themselves to the application of existing law and do not make new law through their innovative interpretation of the old. If existing law is clearly unsatisfactory, it is the business of the legislators, and not the judges, to change it. Given the security of tenure of an independent judiciary, it is not accountable to the people, and since an effective rule of law requires that a government in respect of its exercise of all its sovereign powers be subject to such accountability, then the legislators must be also. From this point of view, it is quite wrong for the Supreme Court in the United States to take it upon itself to decide that abortion is legal when previously it had not been or to decide later that it is not legal.

The legality of abortion should be a matter for the US Congress under rule of law principles. Judges do, of course, have to interpret the law in the light of circumstances that were not and perhaps could not have been envisaged when the law was first made. But it is even questionable whether we should endorse the Supreme Court's decision in the case of Brown vs Board of Education in 1954 that segregated schools were unconstitutional on the grounds that separate schools were inherently unequal and thus could not meet the requirement of the 14th amendment to the constitution regarding citizens' rights to the equal protection of the laws.[3] The consequence of the Supreme Court's usurpation of legislative powers has been to politicize appointments to the court and undermine the separation of powers on which the effective rule of law depends.

My conclusion regarding the extent to which the rule of law is to be understood as a liberal practice is, first of all, that a rule of law regime will primarily benefit those possessing property and liberty rights. The more widely this condition is to be found in a society, the greater the benefits of an effective rule of law will be. Since this condition describes, in effect, a fairly liberal society, the rule of law is not just necessary for the operation of a liberal society but is most attuned to one in the production of its benefits.

In second place, my conclusion is that the rule of law, especially in respect of the subjection of government to law, is unlikely to be created and maintained without the support of practices that are essentially liberal practices and ones that form the content of the subsequent chapters of this book. The rule of law should, then, be seen as much more of an achievement of liberal and democratic regimes than at first appeared. The one partial exception to this conclusion is the sort of regime established in Singapore under the long authoritarian rule of Lee Kuan Yew (1959–90). Singapore under Lee regularly came at the top of the ranking of non-corrupt regimes published by Transparency International in its corruption index. At the same time, Singapore scored poorly on the same organization's democracy index. In this case, it was the strong and effective will of Lee to eradicate corruption in society that enabled him to create a legal system that delivered some features of the rule of law, without accompanying liberal and democratic practices, that made possible the development of a dynamic and prosperous capitalist economy. Strong and authoritarian rulers, however, are much more likely to be corrupt or become corrupted than they are to turn out to be like Lee. So, it is not sensible for a people to entrust arbitrary power to a strong ruler in the hope that he will turn out to be an Akbar or a Lee.[4]

The completion of the rule of law in making government securely accountable may be an achievement of liberal and democratic practices, but liberal regimes can be undermined from within through mounting dissatisfaction by sections of the people with their economic, cultural and demographic situation and through its exploitation by demagogues such as Hitler in Germany and Mussolini in Italy in the 1920s and 1930s. Some people believe that the US President, Donald Trump, will turn out to be another example. Trump has certainly given some signs of incipient authoritarianism. He has denigrated the federal judges who have blocked the operation of his executive order temporarily banning travel to the United States from some Muslim majority countries and called their authority into question. He regularly attacks the mainstream media for dishonesty and the creation of fake news just because they contest his claims and criticize his actions. He calls them, in a sinister phrase, enemies of the people. He frequently expresses his admiration for Vladimir Putin as a strong ruler when the main thing to admire about Putin would seem to be his success in controlling the judiciary, the media and the electoral system so as to ensure that his rule is unchallengeable. These are not good signs from a liberal point of view. But you would expect the liberal and democratic institutions and traditions of the United States to be strong enough to contain him within the bounds that he seems incapable or unwilling to impose on himself.

FURTHER READING

For further reading on the rule of law see Tamanaha (2004), Bingham (2011), Vincent (2012); on China see Fenby (2012); on Russia see Dawisha (2014), Gessen (2012).

A powerful case against rule by the US Supreme Court can be found in Berger (1997).

On managed or illiberal democracies, see Wolin (2017).

NOTES

1 A serf in western Europe was tied to the land he occupied which belonged to his feudal lord for whom he was obliged to work. But he possessed some rights which the lord was expected to defend – such as to occupy that land and maintain himself and his family by working it. Typical patriarchal laws denied women the right to control property or hold public offices, which ensured their subordination to men.
2 Basic Human Rights Instruments (Geneva: Office of the High Commissioner for Human Rights, 1998, pp.31–57).
3 Brown v. Board of Education of Topeka, 347 U.S. 483 (1954). En.m.wikipedia.org.
4 Akbar was the enlightened ruler of the Mughal Empire in the Indian subcontinent from 1556 to 1605.

FREE SPEECH

While I call this chapter "free speech", the fuller statement of the liberal freedom in this sphere is freedom of thought and its expression. Attacks on freedom of thought rather than on its expression have to take the form of inquisitorial procedures forcing a person to confess his inner beliefs. Such inquisitions are obviously outrageous from a liberal point of view, and I shall concentrate on the freedom to express one's beliefs or what is usually called free speech. I shall mean by speech in this chapter any communication by one human being to others through words, pictures or other symbols in the various media of communication such as conversation, public speaking or demonstration, the press, radio, television, post, telephone and the Internet. By freedom I shall mean in the first place the absence of legal penalties for speech. But in the second place, I shall also consider restrictions on speech arising from what J.S. Mill called the moral coercion of public opinion and in particular the operation of what is now called political correctness.[1]

To begin, then, with legal restrictions on free speech. No country, and so no liberal country, allows completely legally unrestricted speech. I shall enumerate the standard areas of restriction and identify the interest of individuals and citizens that is deemed worthy of protection through restrictions on speech. The standard areas are set out in the following sections.

LIBEL AND SLANDER

These restrictions have to do with protecting a person's interest in his reputation as a trustworthy associate. I may be of the opinion that John Smith is a swindler. If I do not communicate this belief to anyone, I do no harm to Smith. But if I start expressing this view of Smith, I become subject to the laws of slander and libel. I would be doing serious harm to Smith's reputation and thus to his fundamental interests in being regarded by others as a trustworthy partner in social interactions. In my view, it should be sufficient to defend the expression of my belief that Smith is a swindler for me to produce the evidence to support it. This would show that, if Smith has a reputation as an honest man, he does not deserve it and should have no redress against me for destroying what he has no right to. In fact, however, the English libel law did not originally recognize truth as a defence because its main concern was to protect the reputation of public figures. Under the present laws, truth and even honest opinion are valid defences.[2]

With regard to defamation, there is a conflict of interest between the interest of one person in being able to speak freely and the interest of another in the preservation of his reputation as trustworthy associate. It is not a case that can be settled by appeal to an equal liberty principle. My being free to rubbish your reputation, unjustly or not, does not restrict your liberty to speak on any subject including by rubbishing mine. The argument for restricting speech in this area must be that unrestricted speech would make it impossible, or too difficult, to maintain the distinction between those who deserve to possess a reputation for trustworthiness and those who don't and that the maintenance of this distinction is in every honest person's fundamental interest as well as being in society's interest in promoting honesty among its members.

INVASIONS OF PRIVACY

Invasions of privacy may be physical, as in entering your private space, to which you have an entitlement, without your permission, or informational, as in publicising information about you, which you have a right to control access to, without your agreement.

I am concerned in this section solely with the latter. Invasion of privacy as a ground for restricting what information others may acquire and publicize about you is different from defamation. The information that another wrongly publishes about me may be true and non-defamatory and yet be an invasion of my privacy. In 2004 the supermodel Naomi Campbell was held by the English courts to have had her privacy invaded by the publication of photographs in the Daily Mirror of her leaving a clinic of Narcotics Anonymous.[3] As it was a true picture, it was not defamatory.

Until the adoption of the European Convention of Human Rights into English law in 1998, English law did not recognize a specific right to privacy but dealt with such matters under the notion of breach of confidence. A right to privacy is now widely recognized. Article 8 of the European Convention affirms a right of respect for one's private and family life, home and correspondence. This is understood to include the right to control the dissemination of information about one's private life, the right not to be subject to unlawful surveillance or the invasion of, or eviction from, one's home. The Convention accepts certain limitations on this right. These are the interests of national security, public safety, prevention of disorder or crime, and protection for the rights and freedoms of others. These limitations must be applied in accordance with the law and be necessary and proportionate. Furthermore, the right to privacy must be balanced against, and may be overridden by, the public interest in free speech, for example when the private sexual or financial life of a public figure may become a matter of legitimate public concern.[4]

Why should privacy be a fundamental interest of persons justifying constraints on freedom of speech? The enjoyment of privacy consists in being able to decide who to allow to participate in aspects of one's life or in the case of solitude whether to allow anyone to do so. Without the right to exclude people, certain forms of life would cease to be possible. There would be no family life, no friendships, no solitude, no private associations or societies. Having to live one's life constantly exposed to the scrutiny of others is one of the nightmares of Orwell's novel, *1984*.

Some people think that we have already arrived at this situation because of the way we have been persuaded by Google, Facebook and others to give them vast amounts of personal information about ourselves which they use to sell to advertisers who can then tailor their advertisements to each person's tastes. "You have zero privacy anyway. Get over it", the chief executive of Sun Microsystems declared.[5] However, the fact is that we have agreed to allow Google and co. to collect and use this information about us to make their vast profits in return for the free use of the services they provide. So, our right to privacy in the form of a right to control the personal information that others acquire about us entitles us to seek to regulate what information they acquire and what they do with it. At the very least we should have the right to access that information and to correct inaccuracies in it.

Organizations that possess personal information about us are now required by law to protect that information from being accessed by unauthorized persons. Furthermore, the European Court of Justice recognizes a right to be forgotten (2014) and requires Google to delete some items about an individual's past unless there is an overriding public interest in others having the right to know about that past.[6] Yet, it appears to be very difficult to erase this information altogether from the Internet. Is this because Google is not complying with the Court's ruling, or is the technology for enhancing privacy in these and other respects not adequately developed? I do not know. What is clear is that our privacy is under threat in the digital age from the vast amount of information about us that both the private internet companies and the government have acquired.

PUBLIC ORDER, PUBLIC HEALTH AND PUBLIC MORALITY CONSTRAINTS

According to the European Convention on Human Rights, speech may be restricted in order to protect public order, public health and public morals. Speech likely to create public disorder, such as mendaciously crying fire in a crowded space or that is an incitement to riot or to commit other criminal acts, is not protected. The interest that is being furthered by public order constraints is the interest of individuals in being able to go about their legal business without the threat of serious harm or disruption. It is their interest as members of a society in peaceful and orderly movement and association.

While the laws on public order can be formulated so widely as to make large public meetings and demonstrations count as threats to public order and hence illegal, I shall discuss the issues that arise from that possibility in the chapter on freedom of association rather than in this section. To make all public protest against government policy and action illegal is certainly the mark of an illiberal regime. But it is better to arrive at this judgement after identifying the points at which liberal and illiberal societies start diverging in matters of restrictions on free speech, which I will be doing shortly.

Restrictions on speech based on considerations of public morality may look as though they should have no place in a liberal regime. But even a liberal regime may reasonably maintain some obscenity laws. While adult pornography that does not involve criminal acts is not restricted in most liberal societies, child pornography is illegal. The principle here seems to be that if the act portrayed is legal, then the pornographic representation of it is legal also. Sexual acts with children are for obvious reasons illegal and hence the pornographic representation of them is too. Also, if prostitution is criminalized, then advertising such services will be illegal as well. However, if a society does not have a liberal attitude to sexual freedom between consenting adults, constraints on free speech arising from public morality concerns could be very substantial. This issue will be discussed at greater length in the chapter on sexual freedom. As for public health concerns as a ground for restricting speech, this would cover the right to control public information in times of pandemics or other serious public health hazards.

CONSIDERATIONS OF NATIONAL SECURITY

Speech that endangers national security is a threat to the fundamental interests of individuals as members of an independent political society in a world of other actively or potentially hostile societies. Constraints on it are obviously justifiable. The problem is that the guardians of national security have to be the government and its security agencies. They can use the claim that there is a threat to national security to expand their secret surveillance of citizens beyond what is reasonable and at the same time obstruct or criminalize the legitimate activities of groups opposed to the existing government's policies. The idea of national security can be extended to include the security of the holders of power, as is standard in contemporary Russia and China and many other parts of the world.

The problem of reconciling the secrecy necessary for the operations of the security services with the transparency and accountability required for the achievement of the rule of law and democratic government has always been present. But modern technology has vastly increased its difficulty because of the incredible amount of data about its citizens that even liberal-democratic governments have themselves collected or have access to through the collections of the private Internet companies and mobile phone resources. The extent of these collections by the US and UK governments has been revealed by the whistleblower Edward Snowden.[7] What is needed at the very least are clear and precise laws detailing the grounds justifying secret government surveillance and at the same time specifying what are unacceptable reasons for such activities, such as to save government from embarrassment, to prevent the disclosure of government wrong-doing, to promote the entrenchment of a particular ideology or the suppression of political or industrial unrest. Other formal measures are parliamentary oversight of the security services by special committees supported by expert advisers and the use of the independent judiciary to decide whether a particular exercise of surveillance is justified by the laws, although that will have to be done in secret hearings. But it cannot be doubted that this is an area in which the establishment of government accountability is very insecure.

THE DIVERGENCE BETWEEN LIBERAL AND ILLIBERAL SOCIETIES ON FREE SPEECH

I have so far in this chapter been identifying those standard constraints on free speech that are common to both liberal and illiberal societies together with the interests that justify those constraints. In some cases, illiberal societies will interpret the principle justifying a degree of constraint, such as national security, public order or public morality, in much broader terms than would a liberal society. However, underlying that broader interpretation will be differences in the society's attitudes to the proper scope of freedom in matters of morality or free speech. I shall now discuss the scope of free speech in societies widely accepted as liberal ones, such as the United States, the UK, Canada, France and the other countries loosely associated as the west.

The liberal societies, then, allow complete freedom of speech, with the exception of the above-mentioned constraints and in some cases the category of hate speech, on all matters political, moral, religious, scientific, historical, ethnological, racial and sexual, including social and political institutions, government policies and appointments and so on. In short, so long as the speech cannot be brought under one or other of the constraining principles, narrowly interpreted, and does not fall into the category of hate speech, the law will protect it.

This understanding of the liberal conception of free speech is expressed in the International Covenant on Civil and Political Rights, which I have already referred to in Chapter 2 as having the status of international law. It affirms in its article 19 that:

1 Everyone shall have the right to hold opinions without interference.
2 Everyone shall have the right to freedom of expression; this right shall include freedom to seek, receive and impart information and ideas of all kinds regardless of frontiers either orally, in writing, in print, in the form of art or through any other media of choice.

The article allows restrictions on these rights only if they are provided by law and are necessary for a) the respect for the rights and reputation of others and b) the protection of national security or of public order or of public health and morals.

Furthermore, most states have constitutions which grant its citizens the above freedoms. For instance, the People's Republic of China asserts in article 35 of its constitution that "citizens of the People's Republic of China enjoy freedom of speech, of the press, of assembly, of processing and of demonstration". Yet, its practice contradicts the international norms and its own national commitments.[8] The state controls the main media organizations and bans from public or Internet use all mention of the following subjects: democracy, the free Tibet movement, Taiwan as an independent country, the Tiannamen Square massacre, the 2014 Hong Kong protests, the Arab Spring, certain religious organizations, and anything questioning the legitimacy of Communist Party rule in China.

A liberal polity, such as the UK, would, and in fact does, allow discussion of the equivalent topics: e.g. communism; the independence of Scotland; the cession of Northern Ireland to the Irish Republic; the miners' strike and riots of the 1980s; the Brixton race riots; anti-capitalist, anti-liberal, anti-western and religious or anti-religious opinions and organizations of all kinds.

Other states such as Putin's regime in Russia achieve state control of speech by eliminating the independent media and intimidating journalists and opposition leaders through politically motivated criminal prosecutions, and physical attacks including probably murder.[9] Muslim majority states do not protect free speech in matters of religion. Speech critical of Islam or the Koran is standardly subject to blasphemy laws for violation of which the penalty can be severe, including execution.[10] Although the international and indeed national norms appear to mandate a world-wide liberal order of free speech, these norms are as widely disregarded as those concerning the rule of law.

I distinguished earlier between a narrow and a broad interpretation of the permitted restrictions on free speech regarding national security and public order and morals. A broad interpretation understands by national security and public order the state as constituted by the present regime. Thus, the practice of the People's Republic of China treats threats to Communist Party rule and to the inclusion of Tibet and Taiwan as part of China as threats to the national security of China. If the liberal UK state were to adopt this broad interpretation, it would consider criticisms of liberalism and democracy as attacks on the security of the UK. But this identity is untenable. The UK is first and foremost an independent political society and only secondarily a regime of a certain kind. It may choose to order its affairs according to liberal norms or according to communist ones. The choice of regime does not affect its fundamental status as an independent political society. Thus, the narrow interpretation is the only coherent one, and what the People's Republic of China and other illiberal states are doing is not, in effect, adopting a broad interpretation of the free speech restrictions but disregarding the free speech norms themselves.

It is a mark of the liberal order of free speech, then, that it permits dissent regarding its own norms. It allows attacks on free speech itself as well as on liberalism and democracy more generally. What it cannot, and does not, permit is speech that is intended to incite its hearers to commit criminal acts and is likely to have that effect. J.S. Mill distinguishes between publishing in the press an attack on corn merchants as exploiters of the poor and proposing the expropriation of their property, on the one hand, and haranguing an angry crowd of starving poor in front of a corn dealer's house with a powerful expression of the same opinions, on the other. Mill holds that while the newspaper article should be protected, the latter is an act of incitement to commit violence in circumstances in which violence is likely to occur and cannot for that reason be allowed.[11]

The US Supreme Court endorsed Mill's view in a judgement in the Brandenburg case in 1969. Brandenburg was a leader of the racist organization called the Ku Klux Klan and was filmed at a meeting of the Klan saying that if the US government continued to oppress the white race, revenge might have to be taken. The Supreme Court overthrew Brandenburg's earlier conviction by a lower court on the grounds that advocacy of the use of force or violence should not be proscribed by law "except where such advocacy is directed to inciting or producing imminent lawless action and is likely to incite or produce such action". This so-called Brandenburg rule is now the law in such matters in the United States and is widely discussed in other liberal states.[12] It would seem to me to follow from this rule that Muslim jihadists who publicly advocate the assassination of non-Muslims in circumstances that now exist in which non-Muslims are being assassinated by Muslims all over the world should be prosecuted and imprisoned. It is sometimes objected that this would involve imprisoning people for the expression of "mere words". This is silly. The words in the context are incitements to commit imminent lawless acts of murder and are likely to incite or produce such acts.

HATE SPEECH LAWS AND POLITICAL CORRECTNESS

One important consequence of the Brandenburg rule is that it protects hate speech that does not violate the rule's incitement conditions. Hate speech broadly understood is speech that attacks a person or group on the basis of attributes such as race, religion, ethnic origin, sexual orientation, disability or gender. Most European states have adopted laws criminalizing some forms of hate speech. The UK's Public Order Act 1986 prohibits the expression of racial hatred, which is defined as hatred against a group by reason of the group's colour, race, nationality or ethnic or national origins. A person is guilty of this offence if he uses:

> [t]hreatening, abusive or insulting words or behaviour or displays any written material which is threatening, abusive or insulting if a) they intend thereby to stir up racial hatred or b) having regard to all the circumstances racial hatred is likely to be stirred up.

In 2006 the expression of religious hatred and in 2008 hatred on grounds of sexual orientation were added as criminal offences. (In 2013 the word insulting was removed from the various acts covering the expression of hatred.[13]) Related to hate speech restrictions are laws prohibiting "holocaust denial" (the denial that the Nazis committed genocide against the Jews). Some European states have such laws but not the UK or of course the United States.

These are relatively new restrictions on free speech, and they have been adopted largely by states that are standardly thought of as liberal. So what sort of justification is offered for these restrictions? A widespread view is that members of the groups that are given special protection under these laws are vulnerable minorities whose status as equal citizens is insecure and threatened by hate speech. The laws are, therefore, necessary to ensure that these people can enjoy the equal respect and dignity to which they are entitled. I call this a liberal justification because it is grounded in the values that underlie the liberal polity. It has the same structure as policies of reverse discrimination. Special legal privileges are given to the members of certain groups in the belief that they are necessary to achieve a basic level of equality for all citizens. In effect, this liberal justification of hate speech restrictions involves an appeal to the fundamental liberal idea of an equal freedom. Hate speech, it is claimed, by systematically denigrating the vulnerable minorities, threatens to undermine the conditions of their enjoyment of an equal freedom. Hence, they need special protection.

While the form of this justification may be acceptable because it expresses a commitment to liberal values, the legal restrictions on free speech may, nevertheless, not be sensible and may even be counter-productive. There is first of all a problem with identifying the groups worthy of protection under the hate speech laws. It was originally conceived as combatting racism and related hatreds such as hatred of different ethnic or national groups. But it has expanded to include religion, gender and sexual orientation. Other possible groups for inclusion are the disabled, transgender people, the obese, the aged. At some point, it may be difficult to resist a universal ban on hate speech.

This takes us to the second problem. The hate in hate speech cannot be given an adequately objective definition. Hatred is defined in UK laws as the use of threatening, abusive or insulting words or behaviour or the display of any written material that is threatening, abusive or insulting. While the word insulting has been removed from the UK statutes, what someone finds abusive or threatening is likely to contain a large subjective element. This danger has been compounded by the 1994 insertion of a clause in the original 1986 Public Order Act that makes it an offence if a person displays any writing, sign or other visible presentation that is threatening etc. "thereby causing that or another person harassment, alarm or distress".

Under these acts a Christian carrying a sign saying, "Stop immorality. Stop homosexuality. Stop lesbianism. Jesus is the Lord" was successfully prosecuted and fined in 2001. Clearly some gay person might see these words as abusive and be alarmed and distressed by their negative attitude to his or her sexual orientation. But it is totally ridiculous that a person should be fined for expressing such a view just because someone might be alarmed or distressed by them. The objective threat to a gay person from the use of these words is, in the context of modern Britain, entirely negligible while the threat to free speech by the banning of their public expression is a serious matter. In another case, in 2010, a man who left some anti-religious cartoons in the prayer room at Liverpool airport and was accused by a chaplain of causing him alarm and distress was given a six-month suspended prison sentence and banned from carrying anti-religious material in a public place.[14]

The extremes of subjectivity that these policies are open to has actually taken concrete form on university campuses where so-called "safe places" have been created in which students are protected from being exposed to any critical or negative speech about their beliefs, values or behaviour. At the same time, some student unions captured by the spirit of the hate speech laws have been denying platforms to speakers, invited by a member society, but who are known to have critical opinions of some group deemed by the union to be worthy of protection. Another method of preventing the expression of views held by the students to be objectionable is to disrupt the meeting at which they are due to be delivered. Both methods are entirely unacceptable from the point of view of the liberal practice of free speech.

In these examples hate speech has come to include any critical or negative attitude towards the group to be protected. This may or may not have been intended by the framers of the hate speech laws. But it is very bad news for open and robust discussion of all opinions, beliefs and values, and has turned into a very illiberal feature of these supposedly liberal societies. It has the further consequence of giving a privileged position to the members of the group who appear to be above criticism. This constitutes the third problem arising from these restrictions. Rather than serving to reduce the amount of real hatred and prejudice towards the protected groups, the laws may be counter-productive. Certainly, to go by the amount of utterly despicable prejudice expressed anonymously on the Internet towards these people, the hate speech laws have had no effect on the existence of the sentiments but only on the medium of their expression. The privileged legal position of the groups may well be creating resentment in parts of the population that are in close socio-economic competition with them. There is a political narrative that has recently emerged in the west according to which a populist revolt of the indigenous and white working class has been taking place against a liberal and globalizing elite promoting a multi-culturalist agenda that advances the interests of the protected groups to the neglect of those of the working class.

For these reasons I do not think that the hate speech laws are a good idea. They should be withdrawn or allowed to fall into disuse. At the same time, non-legal norms of civility should be widely followed in public discussions of the beliefs, values and behaviour of different groups. Behaviour that constitutes harassment, intimidation or bullying is, in any case, subject to the law quite independently of hate speech restrictions. But speech that does not violate the Brandenburg rule – that is to say, is not an incitement to imminent lawless action and is not likely to produce such action – should not be legally penalized.

However, norms of civility in this area may be enforced in a process that Mill deplored and called the moral coercion of public opinion. Mill thought of public opinion as illiberal and unprogressive in spirit. Today, the same process is often attacked under the term "political correctness". In effect, political correctness is used to express a negative attitude to the pressure of "enlightened liberal" opinion in promoting what the hate speech laws offer – special protection or consideration for certain groups designated as vulnerable minorities. The United States, which does not have hate speech laws, nevertheless, appears to suffer badly from political correctness. However, Mill is confused in attacking public opinion for its moral coerciveness. There is no way that one can have non-legal norms of civility or non-legal norms of anything else without public opinion supporting them, and without supporting them through a process that must involve in part moral coercion i.e. criticism, blame, condemnation and so on. The only subject up for discussion is what those norms should be. Mill cannot seriously object to the moral coerciveness of public opinion. But he can object to the backward and illiberal nature of the norms endorsed by Victorian England's public. Similarly, when people object to political correctness today, the only legitimate object of their criticism is the type of multi-culturalism being promoted by the current norms.

The norms of civility I have in mind do not have to take the form of this "enlightened" multi-culturalism. They do not have to be expressed as giving special protection for disadvantaged groups. The norms of civility for the public discussion of the beliefs and values of different groups should apply equally to all. In such discussion one should be allowed to express critical and negative attitudes to the beliefs and values of any group without being morally silenced and without being denied platforms by cries of Islamophobe, homophobe, sexist, racist or multi-culturalist, liberal, leftie. One may be one or other of these things, but the norms of civility I have in mind require all parties to give reasons for their views rather than to attempt to intimidate the other by the use of threatening or abusive words.

AN EQUAL RIGHT TO FREE SPEECH

In general, it would seem that one person's right to free speech is unproblematically compatible with everyone else's equal right. But not everyone can speak in the same forum at the same time. Rules for orderly speech have to be adopted, and these rules have to be fair and appropriate to the context in which opportunities for speech are being sought. In many contexts these rules will require aspirants to speak to have suitable qualifications. The right of everyone to hold and express opinions on any subject does not mean that all beliefs, whether about facts or values, are equally reasonable. It means only that a person may hold and express any opinions, subject to the limitations discussed earlier, without being liable to suffer any penalties, except for the scorn merited for the adoption by people who have received an adequate education; of ignorant beliefs, such as that the earth is flat or the centre of the planetary system; or that God created the species immediately rather than through a process of evolution; or that Soviet communism is the best form of polity for human beings.

While equal right cannot mean equal opportunity to speak regardless of contextual qualifying rules, there may nevertheless be problems of access to particular media of expression such as newspapers, television etc. In general, the rich, the powerful and the well-connected will be able to have their opinions expressed more easily than the rest. This raises questions about how to understand the equality principle present in the liberal idea, which I will postpone discussing until Part II.

FURTHER READING

By far the best and fullest treatment of all the subjects discussed in this chapter is Garton Ash (2016). General discussions also recommended are Warburton (2009) and Haworth (2015). On more specific topics, see Gould (2005), Lukanoff (2012), Wacks (2010).

NOTES

1 J.S. Mill's discussion of the moral coercion of public opinion is to be found in his essay "On Liberty" (2015). See in particular p.8 and pp.77–8.
2 Garton Ash (2016, pp.300–1).
3 Barendt (2007, pp.239–41).
4 The European Convention on Human Rights. www.echr.coe.int.
5 Quoted in Garton Ash (2016, p.284).
6 Charles Arthur, "Explaining the 'Right to be Forgotten': the Newest Cultural Shibboleth", *The Guardian*, 14 May 2014, http://perma.cc/DV2F-539Y.
7 Edward Snowden was working as a computer analyst with the US National Security Agency when he copied and disclosed to unauthorized persons vast amounts of secret files revealing the extent of his government's and the government of the UK's surveillance of their subjects. Some people think that he seriously harmed these governments' national security and anti-terrorist programmes; others that he acted in the public interest. He has been charged in the United States with theft of government property and violation of the Espionage Act but currently enjoys asylum in Russia. See Greenwald (2014) and Harding (2014).
8 China signed the International Covenant on Civil and Political Rights in 1998 but has yet to ratify it.
9 Alexander Litvinenko was a British naturalized defector from the Russian secret service. He was murdered in London in 2006 by polonium poisoning. A British public enquiry in 2016 concluded that the murder was a Russian government operation probably ordered by Putin. The Russian government is presumed to have been involved also in the attempted murder by poisoning of Sergei Skripal and his daughter in Salisbury, England in 2018 as well as other deaths. Joel Gunter, 'Sergei Skripal and the 14 deaths under scrutiny', *BBC News*, 7 March 2018.
10 Some 20 states have neither signed nor are parties to the International Covenant on Civil and Political Rights including Saudi Arabia, Brunei, Malaysia, Singapore, Oman, United Arab Emirates.
11 J.S. Mill (2015, p.55).
12 Garton Ash (2016, pp.132–5).
13 Hate Speech Laws in the UK, https://en.m.wikipedia.org.
14 Ibid.

FREEDOM OF ASSOCIATION AND MOVEMENT

FREEDOM OF ASSOCIATION

Freedom of association involves the right of individuals to form associations and to act together to promote the association's interests in various ways including by peaceful assembly and protest.[1] Individuals have the right to join such associations in accordance with their rules and indeed the right to leave them. However, there are standard limits on what associations can be formed and how they can act. These are limits that liberal states recognize as much as non-liberal states.

The limits have to do with whether the purposes and activities of the association abide by the laws. But we need to distinguish between laws which protect the person and property of individuals or collectivities and what I shall call ideological laws. Laws banning all forms of religious association and practice would be an example of ideological laws. So would laws criminalizing all forms of religion except Christianity or Islam or Judaism. However, liberal laws that protect people's rights to practise the religion of their choice are also examples of ideological laws. Of course, ideology will affect exactly what personal and property rights are recognized in a particular state. I discuss the latter in the next chapter. Here my point is to identify associations no state could allow because they are conspiracies to commit violations of the type of laws that every state must have. Every state must have laws that forbid its members from killing or injuring other individuals and stealing or damaging whatever other people or entities have property rights over. The most basic function of the state is to provide such protection for its members. Hence, organizations, such as the mafia, which are aimed at extracting money from others by violence or the threat of violence, are criminal conspiracies that every state should ban. Laws that protect the person and property of members I call non-ideological criminal laws.

However, if the laws of a state make the practice of religion illegal, then it will be a criminal offence to form a religious association. So, in order to distinguish the liberal practice of freedom of association from non-liberal practice, we cannot just say that the limits to the practice of free association are constituted by the legality or illegality of the association's purposes. The liberal practice of free association allows all associations that are not mafia-type criminal conspiracies. It allows associations whose aim it is to change the law and even to change the law by violent means provided that the association's activities do not violate the Brandenburg rule. Thus, the liberal ideological equivalent of an illiberal state's ban on e.g. all religions but one is the enactment of laws protecting the rights of individuals to free speech about religion and free religious association. The liberal state's ideological laws criminalize acts that deny people their liberal rights. But whereas the hypothetical illiberal state makes all religious associations illegal that are not the privileged one, the liberal state will allow associations that are directed at subverting even the liberal laws themselves. Thus, it allows anti-liberal, anti-democratic and anti-capitalist associations to promote their ideas and goals.

The liberal-democratic state would, therefore, seem to be very vulnerable to subversion by illiberal and anti-democratic ideas and movements. Given that such movements will have no compunction in using liberal-democratic institutions to destroy liberal-democracy if they can, and that the liberal state will employ the coercive law to defend itself only at the last moment, so to speak, in the form of the Brandenburg rule, the liberal state must win the battle of ideas in order to retain its legitimacy. Its most powerful weapon in this battle is its control of the education system. It must insist on the teaching in its schools of liberal and democratic principles and values. It is not required to give any time to the teaching of anti-liberal and anti-democratic ideas although it is sensible that its citizens should grow up informed about the ideas of the enemies of their way of life.

The right of the liberal state to prioritize its own beliefs and values over those of its enemies is a right grounded ultimately in the sovereignty of the state and the right of its people to choose the terms of their association. Having chosen how they wish to live together, a people must have the right to teach its successive generations how to carry on that way of life. What is distinctive about the liberal way of life is that it attaches value to free speech about ideas and values of all kinds, including the nature and worth of its own system. It is this high valuation of free speech that determines the shape of freedom of association in a liberal regime. If the members are entitled to hold and express illiberal ideas, then they must be entitled also to associate with and to explore, defend and promote these ideas.

Liberal society should, then, be distinguished by the number and variety of associations that are independent of the state. This is the sphere of what has come to be called civil society. It is a sphere protected by the rules and power of the state enforcing the rights of individuals to associate with whom they please, provided that they do not constitute a criminal conspiracy in the non-ideological sense and are not a threat to national security, public order, health or morals.

Connected with the right of association is the right of peaceful assembly and protest. However, the exercise of this right may come into conflict with considerations of public order. In general, peaceful assembly and protest should not be stopped by the lawful authorities just because it is likely to arouse opposition that could turn violent. It is the turnout of the opposition intent on violence that should not be allowed if any demonstration is to be disallowed. Yet, some marches are intended to provoke hostility among opposed groups, such as the marches of Protestant organizations through Catholic neighbourhoods in Northern Ireland and reciprocal parading activity by Catholics. In such circumstances, it may be reasonable for the authorities to ban them altogether because of the violence they provoke or at least to determine the areas in which they are permitted. A similar case in the United States was decided differently as a result of the judgement of the Supreme Court. In 1977, the National Socialist Party of America was granted permission to hold a march wearing Nazi uniforms and displaying the swastika through Skokie, which was a predominantly Jewish town in Illinois. Although in the end the Neo-Nazi party did not march in Skokie but in Chicago instead, the decision of the Supreme Court of Illinois was based on the free speech rights of the Nazis counting the display of the swastika as a form of speech.

Other standard grounds for restricting rights to free association and assembly are expressed in the International Covenant on Civil and Political Rights. Article 4 allows a state to derogate from the rights of association and assembly in times of emergency when the life of the nation is under threat, while article 21 allows restrictions in the interests of national security and public order and for the protection of public health and morals.

The right of free association involves the right to join associations in accordance with their rules and the right to leave. Problems with the right to join may arise from liberal non-discrimination laws that forbid discrimination on grounds of race, ethnicity nationality, religion and gender. In general, men's clubs must be allowed to reject women and conversely. But what is to be done about transgender people? You would think also that a religious association should be allowed to reject non-believers as members. But not always. In a judgement of the Supreme Court in 2010, the Christian Legal Society of the Hastings College of Law was required to admit as a member someone who refused to attest to the Society's statement of belief in Jesus Christ on the grounds that the Society, as a recognized society of the Hastings College of Law, had to abide by the College's non-discrimination policy.

The right to join and leave should normally include the right not to join an association. But until recently the strength of some labour unions was such that they were able to ensure that a condition of employment in the businesses they controlled was membership of the union. However, the "closed shop" should be thought of as a feature of social democracy and not of liberal democracy.

FREEDOM OF MOVEMENT

A right of individuals to move freely round the territory of the independent political society of which they are members must be limited by the rights of property owners to exclude uninvited persons. Normally, then, one's right is to use the public roads, paths and land as one wishes, subject to one's observation of the rules governing access laid down by the public authorities. These rules should be designed to ensure orderly use of the facility by everyone and not as a means for a repressive regime to keep control of its population. Freedom of movement of this kind must include the right to live where one pleases. This right is, of course, limited by the availability of housing that one can afford and whatever reasonable restrictions exist on establishing new living structures (building houses, camping) in certain areas (flood plains, national parks).

However, free movement may also be restricted by considerations of national security, public order, public health and morals. National security should mean the security of the independent political society and not the security of the regime, and will cover such things as access to military and other security establishments but may include much more in times of war. Public order restrictions are of the kind discussed in the previous section under the rights of assembly and protest, while public health constraints cover the spread of contagious diseases and other public health hazards. Under public morals, restrictions on using the public streets and parks by prostitutes for soliciting customers may be adopted. Restrictions of movement on grounds of public morals may be vastly extended in order to maintain the dependence of women on their male relations or men more generally. Thus, in some Muslim countries they are not allowed to enter public spaces unless accompanied by a male relative. Demanding dress codes for women is another device restricting their access as individual women rather than as anonymous black apparitions to the public arena. Insofar as a liberal society is committed to the equal status and rights of women and men, these constraints on women's freedom to access public spaces are a badge of illiberalism.

An extensive freedom of movement limited only by these considerations narrowly interpreted is fundamental to individuals' exercise of their rights to free speech and freedom of association, and is an essential aspect of their being in control of their own lives. It is also necessary for the proper functioning of free markets in labour and capital. Workers must be able to move around in search of the best opportunities for the exercise of their talents, and employers must be able to decide where to employ their capital and to attract labour to such locations. Such freedoms and their limits will be discussed more fully in the next chapter.

Free movement of citizens of a liberal independent political society standardly includes the freedom to travel not only within the country but to leave and return to the country as one pleases. However, even liberal societies now require its citizens who wish to travel abroad to carry with them an official passport. This passport may be withdrawn on grounds of threats to national security or criminal activity by its possessor.

Many countries, even liberal ones, require its citizens to carry identity cards which they must present to the authorities on demand and also to register with them any change of address. The introduction of such measures in the UK has been strongly resisted as constituting illiberal controls of citizens' movements. Liberal governments that have adopted such measures may, in fact, have impeccable records of not interfering with the free movement of their citizens. But the measures do give them access to the means to exercise greater control of their populations, should they become so inclined. They can be used as a system of internal passports, as in China today, to control the movement of the population from the countryside to the cities. Illiberal governments everywhere are disposed to adopt such measures because they fear internal disorder and consequent threats to their regimes.

Freedom of movement across borders is another matter altogether. States do not have to permit unrestricted access to their territory to foreigners. Although a liberal state will allow its members freedom to travel abroad for business or pleasure, other states are not required to admit them. It is their prerogative as sovereign states to decide who may enter their territory and on what terms. An alliance of states such as the European Union may collectively decide to allow freedom of movement to the members of each state of the Union across all their territories. But the subsequent movement of populations has caused serious antagonisms and has contributed to the decision of the British people to exit the Union. Some liberal thinkers believe that the standard international restriction on free movement is profoundly wrong and that the individual's right of free movement must extend across the world and involve open borders. Such people do not understand that the existence of states and their rights is still essential to the enjoyment of whatever international order and international rights individuals may actually have access to.

However, states have agreed to adopt the 1951 United Nations Convention on Refugees, which is now accepted as part of customary international law. Under this convention states have agreed to take in and accord certain rights to refugees and not to return them to their country of origin unless the cause of their becoming refugees has disappeared. A refugee is defined in article 1 of the Convention as a person who is outside their country of nationality or habitual residence; has a well-founded fear of being persecuted because of their race, religion, nationality, membership of a particular social group, or political opinion; and is unable or unwilling to return to their country for fear of persecution. The Convention was originally intended to cover European refugees created by WWII and its aftermath but has been subsequently extended without limit of time or geography.

At the present time, rich countries in Europe, the United States and Australasia are being flooded with people trying to migrate there. Most of these people are not refugees but migrants seeking a better life in richer and more stable countries. There is no duty on states to accept such migrants. There is every right to return them to their country of origin. Some of those seeking to enter the rich countries are fleeing the violence of civil and other wars. Such people would seem to be refugees in any normal sense. But they do not necessarily satisfy the UN definition of a refugee, for they may not be being persecuted for their race, religion etc. They may just be trying to escape being blown to bits in the violence of war. Others are genuine UN type refugees. My guess is that they constitute the smallest proportion of the vast numbers seeking entry to rich countries. War refugees should obviously not be returned immediately to the war zone they were escaping from. But, at some point, the war will come to an end and these refugees should be helped to return and re-establish themselves in their country of origin. There is no duty on the host states to accept and attempt to integrate them as permanent members of their population. Although what is not their duty, they may choose to do anyway.

FURTHER READING

On freedom of association and assembly, see Jarman (1997), Mead (2010).
On freedom of movement, see Barry and Goodin (1992), Pecoud (2010).
On refugees, see Betts and Collier (2017).

NOTE

1 The rights to freedom of association and peaceful assembly are affirmed in the United Nations Covenant on Civil and Political Rights in articles 21 and 22.

ECONOMIC FREEDOM

The freedom in question is the right of individuals to use their mental and physical powers (their personal assets) and whatever other assets they rightfully own as they please subject to certain limitations. There are two substantial qualifications here to individual economic freedom which need to be explained: first, how to determine what constitutes rightful ownership of non-personal assets, and second, the limitations on the use of rightfully owned assets. It may be that rightful individual ownership of non-personal assets is extremely limited and/or the rights to use such assets as one pleases is extremely limited. However, the fundamental right would seem to include the right to sell one's labour power and to buy that of others. Only the most extreme form of collectivist socialism denies these freedoms altogether on the basis of the communist slogan "from each according to his ability, to each according to his needs".[1] The 1945 Labour government in the UK, which was certainly a socialist one, only aimed at controlling the commanding heights of the economy and allowed small and medium scale private enterprise to operate.

So-called free markets in labour and other assets, nevertheless, could not function in an orderly manner without some degree of regulation by an authority. The most standard limitation on such economic freedom, which all law-abiding societies cannot fail to recognize, is the illegitimacy of gaining control of other people's assets by force (or the threat of force) or by fraud. The possibility of a practice in which everyone has an equal right to use her assets freely requires that securing other people's assets must come about with their free consent and not through force or fraud. Contracts of slavery whereby a destitute person sells himself into slavery in return for food and board are also standardly not recognized. It is assumed thereby that no one can rightfully be in the position of having to sell himself into slavery in order not to starve. The condition of slavery is, indeed, illegal under international law, although there still remain significant amounts of de facto slavery or indentured labour in the world, not to speak of its re-legitimation within the territories controlled by the assassins of Islamic State. There will also be public order and national security constraints on how individuals exercise their economic freedom, and the government would have to levy taxes on people's property in order to maintain its basic services of law and order.

A society in which these were the only limits on individuals' economic freedom would satisfy some people who call themselves, and are standardly called, libertarians. In such a society, individuals would be liable in law for the injuries they do to the person or property of others or for breach of contract. But the government would take no steps to protect or promote the general welfare such as a prosperous economy, the public health, housing and education, or to support the poor and destitute. Individuals would be expected to provide for themselves and their families' needs or otherwise to depend on the private benefactions of others. However, no society today is libertarian in that extreme sense. Even the freest economically, such as Singapore, have their governments provide education services and public housing. Libertarianism is usually contrasted today with liberalism. But this is a mistake. It should be seen as a form of liberalism. This is because it is an expression of the liberal idea of a society organized on the basis of the members' equal rights to freedom. I believe it is far from being the best conception of a liberal society. Why I think it is defective will become clear in Parts II and III of the book. But I can say already that the defects stem from its failure, first, to recognize that the individuals contemplating the organization of their society on a liberal basis are already embedded in a community as members of an independent political society, and second, to understand the implications of the equal status of those members.

The rest of this chapter will be concerned with other limitations on economic freedom that are to be found in societies that are usually regarded as liberal ones. In the first place, then, liberal states standardly put government money into activities that are justifiable from the point of view of the liberal state's character as a state rather than its character as a liberal state. They put money into national sports teams, into the arts, into education at all levels from elementary to advanced, and into promoting economic growth. These activities are no doubt good things. But putting government money into promoting them involves raising taxes by taking part of the property of its citizens. This appropriation must count as a constraint on the citizens' economic freedom. They cannot do what they please with the part of their property that the government takes in taxes. These good causes look as though they have nothing to do with liberalism. They limit the freedom of the citizens for the sake of their being able to participate in the national well-being arising from sporting success, aesthetic or intellectual achievement and economic prosperity. These are interests of the citizens of states as such and thus also interests of the citizens of liberal states. Hence, the taxes raised to satisfy them may be justifiable on that basis. However, a specifically liberal justification for some of these expenditures is possible and will be discussed later. How much money should the state be allowed to take from its citizens for such purposes will be an important ground of disagreement between various parties of citizens in liberal states.

In the second place, most contemporary liberal states have regulations that limit the freedom of workers and employers to enter into contracts that in the opinion of the state are seriously detrimental to the interests of the workers. There are regulations governing health and safety conditions of work, maximum working hours per day or per week, minimum wages, unfair dismissal and trade union recognition. On the face of it, these regulations are paternalist in character. It is assumed that the workers have insufficient bargaining power to protect their reasonable interests in decent and fair conditions of work and that employers will either exploit their weakness or will be driven by competition among themselves to adopt the worst practices. So the state should step in to ensure conditions of work that the workers would insist on themselves if they had the power to do so. Paternalist legislation, as we shall see in Part II, is not in the spirit of liberalism. But the liberal gloss on these worker protection practices is precisely that they are necessary to level out the playing field sufficiently to enable workers to protect and promote their fundamental interests when operating in otherwise free markets.

Consumer protection laws also restrict the freedom of entrepreneurs and the beneficiaries of the laws – the consumers. In the UK, there are laws that prohibit contracts for the purchase of goods or services that are particularly onerous on the purchaser and hence are deemed unfair. Others regulate product safety to ensure that what the consumer purchases is not a danger to him. There are financial regulations designed to protect consumers, who borrow money in order to finance their purchases, from entering into contracts whose terms they do not understand. Such laws are like worker protection laws in being paternalist in character. They assume that without them consumers would be exploited by less than scrupulous business people. Consumers are inclined not to read all the small print of the contracts to buy that they enter into so that it is easy and tempting enough for the seller to include obviously unfair clauses. With regard to safety regulations, it is difficult for the average consumer to assess the dangers of many of the products that she buys. Well-designed and enforced laws will reduce avoidable accidents and increase consumer confidence in the products available.

A libertarian would object to such paternalism: it should be up to the buyer of goods and services to decide for herself whether what is on offer is fair or risky. The principle that should apply for the libertarian is caveat emptor – let the buyer beware. Consumer protection laws necessarily limit the operation of the caveat emptor principle. Can they be given a liberal gloss? Yes, if an appeal is made to the level playing field idea. If the consumer is expected to look out for himself in regard to all the contracts to buy that he enters into, he would have to employ experts to advise him on the terms being proposed and the safety of the goods he is interested in buying. This will increase his costs in time and money. He will be inclined to take risks. The seller can exploit this while facing no risks of his own. The protection laws thus make the initial contract situation fairer. Furthermore, in facilitating the consumer's purchases, the legislation can be said to promote consumption and thereby benefit sellers in general.

The consumer is also protected from exploitation by effective anti-monopolistic and anti-cartel legislation. Monopolies arise when one enterprise has become the sole seller or buyer in a market. When faced with many consumers of its product (if a seller) or many sellers (if a buyer), it is in a position to impose terms on the many that will maximize its advantage at their expense. The monopolistic seller can raise the price of its good albeit by restricting the supply at the same time. It will do this if it can thereby increase its overall profit. The many buyers will have been disadvantaged by having to pay a higher price for, and enjoy a smaller quantity of, the good than they would have done if competition between several firms had existed. Cartels arise when a small number of firms can by working together achieve a monopolistic position in the market enabling them to raise prices and restrict supply. The most famous cartel in recent years has been OPEC when its members controlled the greater part of the world market in oil production. With the rise of non-OPEC oil producers and especially with the emergence of significant amounts of shale oil production in the United States, OPEC's power to control the market for oil has disappeared. Some monopolistic situations are more or less unavoidable, as is the case with utilities such as the railways and water supply companies, or are susceptible to cartelization as in the energy supply industry. Here the companies can either be taken into public ownership or subjected to a strict regulatory regime designed to protect the consumer.

Anti-discrimination laws constitute another type of constraint on the economic freedom of individuals and businesses. Businesses cannot refuse employment or service to anyone on grounds of sex, race, religion, nationality, political affiliation, age or sexual orientation. Such laws are to be found in liberal states and are indeed fundamental to the liberal understanding of the equality of the citizens and their equal rights. In a recent case in the UK, a Christian couple running a bakery were successfully prosecuted for refusing to bake a cake for customers who wanted decorations on the cake celebrating their gay marriage. Such decorations offended the couple's Christian convictions about the nature of marriage. However, in a similar case in the United States, the Supreme Court ruled in favour of the baker.[2]

A further reason for imposing constraints on individuals' economic freedom of action is based on the idea of public goods. One standard economic argument for "free" markets is that they normally produce better outcomes in terms of the satisfaction of individuals' preferences than does collective provision. However, economists recognize that in some instances free markets will fail to produce this desirable result. The classic case is that of a public good. Examples of public goods are clean air, street lighting, sewage systems and other public health measures, police protection, national defence and so on. The essential characteristics of a public good are non-rivalry and non-excludability. Non-rivalry means that one individual's enjoyment of the good (e.g. clean air) doesn't reduce the amount available to others. Non-excludability means that, once the good is provided, one cannot exclude anyone from enjoying its benefits (where clean air is provided one cannot prevent anyone in the area from enjoying it). Under these circumstances individuals would have no economic incentive to provide the good because they could not ensure that only those who were willing to pay for it received the benefit. If payment were voluntary, most people would become free riders. That is to say they would happily enjoy the good without contributing to the costs of its provision. Hence, if such goods are left to free markets (e.g. free individual action) to provide, they will not be provided at all or only at levels well below what the same individuals actually and reasonably desire. The obvious solution to this problem is to compel all those benefiting from the good or service to contribute to its costs, for example by taxing the residents of the area for which the clean air, street lighting, police protection, national defence and so on are provided. Other methods may be used such as, in the case of pollution, penalizing the polluters or imposing regulations that eliminate the problem. All such methods, however, involve compulsion and so restrict economic freedom.

Nevertheless, if one allows for a broader interpretation of freedom, one can say that justified collective provision is compatible with that broader version. What I have in mind is the idea that one should not be subject to a coercive authority that cannot be reasonably understood as grounded in one's own will for one's good. Thus, in the case of market failure, the claim is that individuals' preferences are not being satisfied. They can be satisfied, however, if the individuals together create an authority that will provide the good desired by everyone and impose a coercively backed charge to pay for its provision which ensures that potential free riders are deterred. In other words, each person can reasonably accept the coercion as an essential part of the arrangement whereby the good can be provided and his interests satisfied.

Clear cases of public good provision by a coercive collective authority may be understood, then, as justifying constraints on individual freedom if the outcome cannot be obtained through individual provision and can be seen as what the individual himself reasonably desires for his own good. However, much of welfare state provision in regard to health, education, unemployment and housing is not such a clear case. For instance, compulsory health and unemployment insurance and pension provision schemes funded through national insurance programmes or out of general taxation look as though they are imposed on people for their own good, because left to themselves they would not provide for their future misfortunes although they were well enough off to do so. If this were the reason for the compulsion, it would seem to be a paternalist measure in conflict with the idea that people should take responsibility for their own lives.

There are, however, two aspects to these schemes: one is the compulsory element and the other is a redistributive element. The compulsory element can be seen in pure form in the case of compulsory motor insurance. Anyone who drives a car must take out insurance against accidents. But the insurance is provided by private companies. The state provides the compulsion and the market the insurance. The compulsion is the apparently illiberal, paternalist measure. The individual is not left to decide for himself whether to insure or not. A reasonable justification for this compulsion is that the uninsured drivers impose additional costs on the insured to cover their potential losses from accidents caused by the penniless uninsured. This imposition is unfair. Hence, it is reasonable for the insured to insist that everyone be insured. The insured would also have the burden imposed on them of caring for those uninsured who are ruined and disabled by their improvidence and might reasonably require compulsory insurance to protect themselves from such demands. Hence, although compulsory motor insurance does involve an element of paternalism in forcing people to insure for their own good, it is more a matter of defending the interests of the provident from the imposition of unfair burdens.

In the case of health, unemployment and pensions insurance the redistributive element complicates the issue. The reason why many would not voluntarily insure against probable future needs is that they are too poor to take out any or an adequate level of insurance. The schemes are, thus, compulsory and redistributive.

Clearly, some people would not insure, or not insure adequately, even if they were financially in a position to do so. For them compulsion is a paternalist measure. Could the insurers justify compulsion because of the costs that the uninsured impose on them? These would be the costs of dealing with the level of poverty and destitution caused by the improvidence of the uninsured. But since it was the uninsured's own fault that they have become destitute, are the insured under any obligation to help them? Yes, they are under obligations of charity to help the impoverished of their own society even if it was the impoverished's own stupidity that brought them to such a condition. A better way of dealing with that obligation, however, would be to prevent the situation arising in the first place by requiring everyone to insure, as is the case with compulsory motor insurance. Thereby, you bring about a world in which no one falls below a level of welfare that is sufficient for everyone to be able to protect and promote her fundamental interests in operating in a free market.

The redistributive element in actual national insurance schemes is also necessarily compulsory. The better off are compelled to contribute to the insurance needs of the worse off. The liberal justification for this is the same. A liberal society needs its members to be financially in a situation in which they can act as independent agents taking responsibility for their own lives. The welfare state provides the background conditions under which it is reasonable to expect one's fellow citizens to commit to liberal principles of interaction even if those conditions can be achieved only through a degree of compulsion.

The combination of compulsion and redistribution is present also in the case of state education provided for out of general taxation. The liberal justification for this is grounded in the belief that every normal adult has the capacity to take responsibility for her own life through the development of the understanding and skills that will enable her to maintain an independent life for herself and her family. However, prior to state provision, large numbers of children received little or no education at all because their families were too poor to be able to afford it. What is at issue here is that the presumed natural capacity of each person to decide for herself what to believe and how to live does not, in the circumstances of a large, complex and scientifically based society and economy, just emerge fully developed in each person without any formal education. A liberal society is not going to be defensible if large numbers of its members, who have the capacity to be self-determining, cannot adequately exercise it because they have not had the opportunity to develop it. The point is not that education is something that the state must provide for all its members. It is conceivable that the necessary education could be provided privately. What is necessary from a liberal point of view is that the state should ensure that everyone receives an adequate education to enable her to protect and promote her fundamental interests while operating in free markets, and to fund this through public provision if it is necessary to achieve the liberal goal.

However, another argument for the state provision of education is that an educated workforce is of benefit not just to the individuals themselves in enabling them to care for themselves and thereby to society in not having to provide for them, but it also creates positive externalities through the contributions each makes to the effectiveness and prosperity of the economy as a whole.

It is reasonable to suppose that, if this adequate education for all is not provided by the state, it will not be forthcoming from private sources. For one thing the positive externality argument shows that education has elements of a public good. If education provision were left to the market mechanism, not enough would be provided. Too many would be left with very inadequate levels of education or none at all under a fully private system. It is true that under a state system in the UK and some other countries, too many are left with a very inadequate level of education. But this does not seem to be the case everywhere, neither does it seem plausible that rich states like the UK cannot provide a public education that gives to all its citizens a level of literacy and numeracy that would enable them to look after themselves as independent members of society.

It may still be wondered whether a liberalism that attributes to people the natural capacity to take responsibility for their own lives is coherent in substituting the community's collective care for the responsibility of parents just in case they should fail to look after their family adequately. Why should the other members of the community bear the costs of such actual or potential failure? If collective provision is necessary, does this not show that the liberal belief in everyone's capacity to take responsibility for their own, including their young children's, lives is unsustainable? Too many would fail. However, in the case of education we are concerned with future citizens who are to become self-determining adults in their own right. If the community is to be in a position to claim their allegiance to liberal norms, it must give them a fair opportunity to come to understand and satisfy their fundamental interests through interacting with other members in free markets. Only then can the community expect them to endorse the liberal practices. So the community itself has a fundamental interest in providing the conditions under which the continued allegiance of successive generations to its liberal ethical character can be maintained.

Contemporary liberal societies for the most part defend the economic freedom of their members – their right to use their mental and physical powers and the other assets they rightfully own as they please in buying and selling goods and services – within the limits of the freedom-restricting practices described earlier. I have suggested why liberal societies might want to embrace such limits on their members' freedom. There is, however, another freedom-limiting practice that is widely advocated and to some extent followed in liberal societies. This is the practice of levying high rates of tax on the better off members, not in order to fund welfare provisions but to promote equality. Whether such a practice can be justified within liberalism depends on what a liberal understanding of the equality of the members involves. My account of that issue will be developed in the chapter on the value of equality in Part II. That account will bear also on the question of what assets, other than her mental and physical powers, can an individual be said rightfully to own and thus legitimately use in entering into trading relations with others.

Liberal economic freedom, as I have been describing its nature and limits, involves the right to possess full private property rights both in personal goods and in the means of production. Private property should be understood as a bundle of rights consisting in the rights to possess, use, manage and derive income from some good together with the power to transfer or waive the right, to exclude others from the possession, use etc. of the good and the liberty to consume or destroy it. A person may possess some of these rights and not others. She may enjoy the rights of possession, use, management and income but not the right to transfer or waive those rights or consume or destroy the good. A person who owns a Grade I listed house in the UK cannot consume or destroy the property and cannot even make any alterations to it without authorization. Rights of way over one's property may be held by the general public or particular people so that the owner has no right to exclude them from that part of her land.

Such limitations are of particular importance in the case of the self-ownership that underlies liberal economic freedom. Under economic liberalism a person is said to have a right to use her mental and physical powers as she pleases subject to the sort of limitations discussed. She has such a right because her powers belong to her. She owns them. But self-ownership of one's natural powers does not mean that all the rights in the bundle described earlier are included in that ownership. One has the right to possess, use, manage and derive income from, by hiring out, one's powers, but one does not have the right to transfer the powers to another by enslaving oneself or the right to sell off one's body parts. Why such limitations on self-ownership are integral to economic liberalism will be discussed when I explore the liberal values of freedom and autonomy in Part II.

Socialists used to believe that no individual should be allowed to own the means of production of others. So while they might accept that individuals owned their own powers and could use them to obtain an income, they could use this income only to acquire personal property in things such as clothes, a home and so on. The means of production, transport and exchange, or at the very least the commanding heights of the economy, should be collectively owned. The Marxist objection to the private ownership of the means of production rests on the claim that this is the way the capitalist extracts the surplus value the worker produces from his labour. Since surplus value is what the worker produces, its appropriation by the capitalist is the measure of the capitalist's exploitation of the worker. Surplus value arises from the fact that the worker produces more value through his work than he costs the employer in wages. However, the idea of surplus value rests on a flawed conception of how the level of wages is determined in the capitalist market – by the costs of reproducing this labour over time and so by the costs of subsistence for the worker and his family. Hence, the worker's position cannot improve under capitalism and he cannot share in the benefits of economic expansion.[3]

Since this is not a very good theory, I shall treat the socialist objection to the private ownership of the means of production to be an objection to the inequality of power between capitalist and worker that results from capitalist ownership. How serious an objection this is depends on one's view of what the liberal belief in the equality of members of an independent political society requires. Once again, this discussion will have to be postponed to the relevant chapter in Part II on the liberal value of equality. But on the face of it, the socialist objection to the inequality between capitalist and worker is an objection from within a liberal perspective and so must be taken seriously by the liberal. She tries to deal with it through vigorous attacks on monopolies and the promotion of competition between enterprises so that the worker has plenty of choice and is not dependent on a single employer. This policy is supported by the kind of worker protection legislation discussed earlier and by worker representation on company boards. Another way is by building up the countervailing power of the workers through trade union organization. But when this takes the form of a corporatist state in which economy and polity are dominated by the organized power blocs of unions and employers, the liberal freedoms will be squeezed because they have to be exercised to accord with the interests of the corporations. The worst possible model for overcoming the inequality of power of worker and capitalist is the Soviet one in which private ownership is superseded by collective ownership through the state. For in that model all economic, political and ideological power is concentrated in the hands of a small elite (or even worse the leader of such an elite) who claim to be representing the interests of the working people. In this system, there are no laws or institutions, no set of rights, that can be invoked to protect anyone against the arbitrary and unaccountable power of the ruler. From a liberal perspective, the Soviet model is sheer lunacy and to no liberal's surprise has led, where it has been adopted, to the most appalling crimes against the people whose interests the system is supposed to be promoting.

FURTHER READING

On slavery in the modern world, see Kara (2017).

On public goods, see "Public Goods: A Brief Introduction, The Linux Information Project". www.linfo.org/public_good.html.

On the nature of property rights, see Honore (1961).

On welfare or social liberalism in general, see the classic "new" liberal work by Hobhouse (1964 [1911]). Also Freeden (1978) and Merquior (1991).

NOTES

1 Endorsed by Karl Marx in his Critique of the Gotha Programme.
2 For the UK case, see www.theguardian.com/uk...gay-marriage-cake-ashers-bakery-northern-ireland; while for the US case see www.theguardian.com/.. gay-cake-ruling-supreme-court-same-sex-wedding.
3 K. Marx (1990, Chap. 8).

SEXUAL FREEDOM

The liberal project to leave adult human beings as free as possible to run their own lives suggests that liberal societies should leave adult sexual relations unregulated by law. Since under that project everyone must enjoy the same freedom, this would mean that consensual sexual relations between adults would be legally unrestricted. This is, in fact, more or less the position in contemporary Europe and the United States. However, consensual incest is still criminalized in the UK and the United States but not in many European countries. It is, nevertheless, generally considered morally unacceptable. Another exception, at least in the UK, is sado-masochistic sexual activity. But even there the decision by the UK's highest court was based on the harm done by the physical assaults in the case rather than on the sexual part of the action. What was banned by the judges was the sado-masochism involved, not the sex.[1] Other liberal jurisdictions focus on the consensual nature of the sado-masochistic exchange and allow it. The legal freedom of adult consensual sex does not, of course, apply to children who are deemed to be in need of protection in these matters. It applies also only to private sexual acts, not to sexual acts performed in public. The latter are offences against public morals.

Historically, however, most societies had laws penalizing extra-marital sex, homosexuality, adultery and fornication. Homosexuality was decriminalized in the UK only in 1967. In the United States laws against it in the various states of the Union were declared unconstitutional by the Supreme Court only in 2003. In other European states it was decriminalized in the course of the 19th and 20th centuries. Indeed, Europe, the U.K. and several US states have gone well beyond mere decriminalization in the direction of treating homosexuality on an equality with heterosexuality by outlawing discrimination and recognizing gay marriage. However, Russia has recently enacted an anti-gay promotion law that is being followed by several other post-Soviet Union states. Furthermore, outside the liberal societies, there is still widespread discrimination against homosexuality. There are over 70 states in the world in which it is still a crime and especially in Islamic law countries can be subject to severe punishment.[2]

The situation with regard to adultery laws is that they disappeared in the UK from 1857 and in other European countries from the 19th century onwards, but in Belgium only in 1987, in Switzerland in 1989 and in Austria in 1997. In the United States such laws remain on the statute books in 21 states and as recently as 2001 a man was successfully prosecuted in Virginia for the crime and fined USD125. However, these laws are not usually enforced. By contrast in Islamic law countries such as Iran, Saudi Arabia, Pakistan and Somalia prosecutions are common and punishments sometimes very severe, including the stoning to death of the convicted.

The attempt by law to control the sexual activity of adults has largely been directed more severely against women than against men. A recent report of the United Nations working Group on Discrimination against Women in Law and Practice focuses on discrimination in adultery laws. It cites the explicit discrimination in the laws of traditionalist societies such as Jewish biblical law and the Laws of Manu of Ancient India in which the crime of adultery consists in sexual intercourse between a married woman and a man other than her husband, and the penalty was imposed on the woman and not the man. A similar attitude was present in the English common law as expressed by the Lord Chief Justice in 1707 when England was liberalizing in other spheres of life.

He states that adultery between a married woman and a man not her husband is a very serious crime involving the highest invasion of property. The reverse situation, in which a married man has intercourse with a woman not his wife, is not said to be a very serious crime. Presumably, if the woman is unmarried it is not an invasion of property at all! The UN report states that in many countries in which adultery remains prohibited, it is similarly understood as consensual sexual intercourse between a married woman and a man not her husband. In contemporary Islamic law countries where there is apparently no discrimination in the statement of the law, nevertheless the law bears more heavily on women than men because men, but not women, are allowed to claim the extra-marital relation as an addition to their wives or concubines and thus is not an adulterous relation at all. Furthermore, in some Islamic jurisdictions such as Pakistan and Somalia, the crime of adultery includes non-consensual sex, thus applying to women and girls who have been raped. The report cites the case of a 13-year-old Somali girl who in 2008 was stoned to death in Kismayo after she had been raped by three men and subsequently convicted of Zina (adultery or fornication) because she was unable to prove her rape claim.[3]

The adultery laws' discrimination against women can be explained in part as an attempt by husbands to assure themselves of their paternity of their wives' children, to protect their property as the English Chief Justice explained it. If the object of the law's concern were adultery simply, why would it discriminate against women? But it is surely also an integral part of patriarchal regimes' efforts to control the behaviour of women in the interests of men. The rise of feminism and the decline of patriarchal laws and norms in western liberal societies are part of the same story as the liberalization of sexual relations. Feminism in its development in the 18th and 19th centuries initially takes a liberal form. Women claim the same rights as are being claimed and accorded to all men. They have the same capacities to take responsibility for their lives and so are entitled to the same rights. Once this view of women begins to spread, it becomes implausible for men to try to control women's sexual activity other than on a basis of equality and mutuality. Of course, it would still be possible to have strict adultery laws applying equally to both sexes. But such strictness for themselves is hardly appealing to most men.

Nevertheless, it is probably true that the liberalization of the norms and attitudes governing sexual relations, as distinct from the laws, that has occurred in western societies in the 20th century was also due to the development of effective and simple contraceptive measures.

Feminism is not essentially liberal in character. There have been socialist forms of feminism, and more recently there has flourished a form of feminism which accentuates the differences between men and women. This different feminism is very critical of liberalism in general for its appeal to the values of rationality and autonomy and its belief in the impersonal forms of law and rights. The construction of the idea of a good society around these values and institutional forms is said to be a male project and unsuitable for women. Women's identity is more closely tied to emotions, feelings and bodily senses and expresses itself typically in an ethics of care and love. This kind of feminism tends to assimilate women's interests to those of cultural minorities and makes the apparently liberal claim that all such groups are due an equal respect. These claims present a problem for liberalism insofar as the values these "minorities" embrace are anti-liberal ones. I will deal with the issues this raises when I come to discuss the claims of such illiberal multi-culturalism in Part II.

The fact that contemporary liberal societies have abandoned the attempt to control the sexual activity of its freely consenting adults by law does not, however, mean that there should not be social norms backed by the moral coercion of public opinion that apply in this sphere. Indeed, some clearly exist, at least in the UK where adultery is widely regarded as a form of cheating and as such is not approved, although the social penalties do not seem to be onerous. Similarly, prostitution is still thought to be degrading, and the prostitutes themselves are for the most part seen as victims. A possible way of grounding such norms is in the interests of successive generations of children. If we accept the evidence that children flourish best as members of a caring family, then this would be a reason for society to adopt sexual norms that promote and protect such groups. (If gay marriage exists, then the norms would apply to such unions also.) It is obvious that it is a major interest of society itself that its successive generations are brought up under the best conditions. So the combined interest of society and its children would provide strong support for such norms.

This line of reasoning supposes that the family is an ethical entity in its own right of a similar but subordinate character to an independent political society. That is to say, once formed, the group acquires a collective authority over its members within its proper domain – the life and interest of the family. Its authority over its children, however, lasts only as long as they remain non-adult members of society. As a matter of fact there will be many such ethical groupings in a liberal society. They are formed through the cooperation of self-determining individuals in pursuit of goods in common. Examples are universities dedicated to the advancement and transmission of knowledge, and trade unions whose members combine to protect and promote their reasonable interests as workers.

FURTHER READING

Weeks (1981) and McWilliams (1993).

NOTES

1 https://en.m.wikipedia.org/wiki/R_v_Brown.
2 According to Asal et al., there were 93 nations in which homosexuality was criminalized when they carried out their studies. V. Asal, U. Sonnor, P. Harwood, "A Cross-National Study of the Legality of Homosexual Acts", *Comparative Political Studies*, 2012.
3 Background information on the statement by the UN Working Group on Discrimination against Women in Law and Practice.

PART II

LIBERAL VALUES

INTRODUCTION

This part of the work is concerned with the interpretation of the main values embedded in or presupposed by the practices described in Part I. These are the distinctively liberal values of freedom and equality and the universal values of community and well-being. There is some dispute as to what the concept of freedom means and why freedom should be valued, and this discussion is thought to affect a person's understanding of what is required by the practice of equal freedom, especially in the economic sphere. With regard to equality, the debate is not so much about the meaning of the concept as about how it is to be understood in its application to fundamental relations between the members of a political society. Here there can be no doubt that the position one adopts on equality determines the kind of liberal regime one is committed to.

The range of possibilities in the interpretation of the practice of equal freedom includes, at one extreme, the so-called libertarian position in which the only governmental constraints on individuals' exercise of their right to liberty are to protect their rights to their person, property and contracts. At the other extreme is an egalitarianism in which the dispute is over whether the equality should be understood in terms of outcomes, such as an equality of happiness or well-being, or an equality of inputs, such as opportunities, capacities or resources. Libertarianism prioritizes free choices and contracts over considerations of equality apart from the initial distribution of an equal freedom. Egalitarianism prioritizes equality of outcomes or inputs over considerations of liberty. Liberty has to be exercised within the constraints of the equal outcomes or inputs. As I take these positions to be extremes, there should also be identifiable intermediate principles.

Part II raises important issues about the understanding of freedom, equality, community and well-being. Some issues will be resolved at this level. Others will not be. But both resolved and unresolved will have to be taken into account in Part III when comprehensive theories of liberalism are introduced. These theories should accept the analysis of the concepts arrived at in Part II and give determinate answers to the unresolved issues. They should tell us why we should understand liberalism from a libertarian or egalitarian perspective or adopt some intermediate view. They should also tell us why a liberal society is morally required or at least is better, all things considered, than the available alternatives.

While freedom and equality are the specifically liberal values that distinguish liberal societies from illiberal ones, they still have to be understood as the fundamental regulative ideas for an independent society that is self-regulating; in other words, for a society that decides what its own social and political arrangements should be.

Such an entity is necessarily a society before it takes a liberal form. One can only have a liberal society if, first of all, there is an independent society and, second, it evolves or adopts a liberal form of organizing itself. As an independent society, a liberal society will have two other fundamental values besides the liberal ones of freedom and equality. These are what I call community and well-being. These are fundamental values of a liberal society because they are fundamental values of any independent society. The value of community refers here to the necessary degree of unity that an independent political society must have to sustain itself as an independent society over time. An independent society is a collection of people who are more or less committed to live together politically: that is to say to live together under common rules and with a common concern for the security and flourishing of their political enterprise. The idea of community in this context is that of the nature and degree of the unity and coherence that a political people must have to survive as an independent entity. While this account looks as though it presupposes a multi-state world full of inter-state antagonisms, in fact it could apply to a world state and its problems in maintaining itself against the forces of disintegration.

The value of the well-being or prosperity of such an entity arises for the members from the fact that as a member an individual is committed to pursuing her interests in her own well-being through the rules and institutions that form the structure of her society. Since the flourishing of the members in general, although not of every particular individual, will be dependent on the flourishing of the whole, the well-being of the whole must be a fundamental value for the members. This consideration must apply to the members of a liberal society also.

I discuss the ideas and values of community and well-being in Part II under the heading "liberal values" when it should be clear that these values are not distinctly liberal ones. But they are necessarily fundamental values for a liberal society. As such, the possible arrangements of a liberal society must be evaluated in their light. That is to say, an interpretation of the practices of an equal freedom that undermined the necessary degree of unity for the society or led to its immiseration could not be viable understandings of freedom and equality for a liberal society.

THE IDEA AND VALUE OF FREEDOM

THE MEANING OF FREEDOM

Some people think that there is an idea of freedom that is purely negative. A person is free if he is not being impeded by other human beings from doing what he wants. They call this freedom from and distinguish it from freedom to do something which is supposed to be positive. This is the initial formulation of Sir Isaiah Berlin's famous essay, "Two Concepts of Liberty".[1] However, a moment's reflection will show that this expression of the distinction between negative and positive freedom is worthless. If I am free from interference from other human beings in doing what I want, there is something I want to do, and hence something positive, that other human beings are obstructing me from doing. The concept of freedom on this view is essentially triadic.[2] There is an X that is free from Y to do Z. Standardly, X is a human being, Y is an action or actions of other human beings and Z is some possible action of X. Even if what I want is to be free from imprisonment and there are no very specific actions I have immediately in mind that I want to do, still what I want is to be free to live a normal life or to do a myriad of things that I could specify if asked why I wanted to be free from prison. To say that I want to be free from something for absolutely no reason makes no sense.

If I am blocked by other human beings from doing what I want, this would appear to be a clear case of unfreedom. However, if I then cease to want to do that thing, my unfreedom will disappear. For this reason, it would be better to express the triadic understanding of freedom in terms of the closing off of a person's options for action. The laws standardly forbid us to do all sorts of things. They close off these things as possible courses of action for those subject to the laws. I may not have seriously considered doing most of these things and may not now want to do any of them. Nevertheless, they are closed off for me as possible actions. I cannot now do them without subjecting myself to the force of the law. The triadic notion of freedom, in fact, allows for the option understanding of freedom since it says only that there is some agent who is free from the actions of other human beings to do some action. It does not say that the agent must want to do the action but merely that the action is available for him to do should he want to do it. It is an option for him.

What we are interested in about freedom in the context of discussions of human socio-political arrangements are the actions of other human beings that prevent a person from doing some action that he may want to do. There may be a sense of freedom in which we can say that a river is not free to flow down its usual course which has become blocked. But this is a metaphorical use of the word and of no interest to us. From this point of view, we should not say a person is not free to swim across a river because he does not know how to swim. His being unable to swim the river is an incapacity of his that probably has nothing to do with the actions of other human beings. Hence, it is not a lack of freedom. However, it is possible that the regime he lives under has made it illegal for its subjects to learn how to swim for fear that they will all swim across the river to freedom! We should, then, say that he is unable to swim the river because he was not free to learn how to swim. Other people have imposed this incapacity on him to stop him from swimming to freedom. So, they have prevented him from even having that option.

When the law forbids me to do something, I may still succeed in doing it by breaking the law. So, although other people tried to prevent me doing the thing, they failed. Hence, I was not prevented and so cannot have been unfree to do it. But what the law does is to prevent me doing what the law forbids without being subject to the credible threat of harms imposed by others. I may escape the harms, but I cannot escape the threats and the unpleasantness of being subject to them.

I may be free from a legal point of view but unable to take up an option that the law allows me because I do not have the money to make the purchase. I am legally free to buy an expensive holiday on South Georgia, but I cannot afford to do so. Is there a sense in which I am not free to holiday on South Georgia? Are any human beings preventing me from doing so or is it my inability to be assimilated to an incapacity such as being unable to swim? Some people talk in this context of my freedom being effective or not. If I am legally free to do X but unable to give effect to my freedom, then I am effectively unfree to do X. However, in that case we would have to say that I am effectively unfree to swim the river although no other human beings are seeking to prevent me directly or indirectly by stopping me learning how to swim. We would have lost the connexion between freedom and the absence of preventive action by other people. Therefore, I think it is better to say that although I am free to swim the river, dine at the Ritz, holiday in South Georgia, those freedoms are not worth anything to me because I can't swim or have no money.

The connexion between freedom and preventive action by others is important. It requires us to think of freedom as something that exists or not in relations between human beings. Suppose what I want – indeed, need – is access to a shelter for the night but have no funds to pay for it. Yet, there are plenty of empty properties around that I could use and I could easily gain forced entry into one of these. But I cannot do this without subjecting myself to the threat of legal action. However, the law is a human creation. It is established and enforced by human beings. Thus, insofar as I am prevented from breaking and entering another's property by the threat of the force of law, it is other people through the law who are closing off that option. In that sense it is correct to say that I am not free to access the shelter that exists. Similarly, I could enter a bank and seize the funds I need for my holiday in South Georgia, but I cannot do that without subjecting myself to the force lurking in the law. The option of taking the funds with impunity that are needed for my holiday is not available to me.

I have been presenting the law as necessarily a restriction on our options and hence our freedom. But these restrictions may be justified in terms of the interests of those subject to them and may indeed increase our options in other respects and thus our freedom. The laws that protect the person, property and contracts of people from force and fraud make possible all the options involved in socially cooperative living. In the words of John Locke, "that ill deserves the name of confinement that hedges us in from bogs and precipices. So that, however it may be mistaken, the end of law is not to abolish or restrain, but to preserve and enlarge freedom".[3] However, I shall not pursue the possible uses of this idea here but will return to it later. Instead, I shall revert to the distinction standardly made between negative and positive notions of freedom and consider whether there is a better way of marking it than the simplistic appeal to the difference between freedom from and freedom to. Berlin, who popularized this distinction in the post-WWII world, expresses the idea of positive freedom in terms of being master of one's own will rather than being directed by others. Negative freedom, then, is not being obstructed or prevented by others from doing what one may want, and positive freedom is the actual doing of actions that spring from one's own will. Positive freedom is self-direction rather than direction by others. The relevant point here is that the triadic notion of freedom that involves the rejection of the difference between freedom from and freedom to as distinct notions of freedom does not contain the positive moment of self-willed action. Freedom to is merely the possibility of an action that is not obstructed by others.

Berlin accepts that there is no great logical distance between the ideas of negative and positive freedom as described earlier. Yet, the distinction is entirely valid and I shall proceed on that basis. However, instead of talking about the idea of positive freedom, I shall refer to it as autonomy. The reason for this is that Berlin's essay publicized and criticized the way in which the idea of positive freedom has been developed in confusing and unattractive directions. He sees the idea of positive freedom as providing a justification for illiberal coercion. If I am positively free only in doing X, then even if I am forced to do X, I will still be free. As Rousseau famously said, I will have been "forced to be free".[4] It became difficult, subsequently, to use the idea of positive freedom with approbation without implying that one endorsed those developments. The idea of autonomy carries none of those implications yet means fundamentally the same thing as positive freedom.

WHAT IS AUTONOMY?

By autonomy I mean the control a person has over his own future states by deciding to do one thing rather than another and by carrying out his decision through the exercise of his will. This control is manifest in short-term and trivial decisions such as choosing to drink a glass of white wine now rather than red wine or something else available to him. But the same power to determine his own future states is present in decisions with long-term trajectories, such as to pursue a legal career or to enter into a marriage. In making and executing such decisions a person is standardly said to be responsible for what she does or becomes. The events of her drinking white wine or marrying Jim are attributable to her as what she has brought about. Autonomy as so understood is a matter of degree in the sense that one can achieve a greater or smaller amount of control over one's future states depending on the present scope of one's decisions. If one's horizon of action does not extend beyond the next few hours, one will be responding to the vicissitudes of the moment and one will have no opportunity to make anything of one's life other than to survive. At the other extreme one may be in a position to make and execute long-term plans that give shape and content to one's distant future. Clearly, the liberal is concerned with autonomy with the greater scope. She wants individuals to take responsibility for what they do or become in their lives in all its important spheres: in regard to sexual partners, occupations, associations and beliefs. But one cannot achieve the ideals of liberal autonomy unless one possesses the power of self-determination, in the first instance, for the short term and the small scale.

Autonomy so understood is equivalent to rational agency – a person's determination of her actions and beliefs by reasons such as her decision not to accept an invitation because of her tiredness, or her choice of legal career because of her love for the courtroom battle, or her commitment to liberalism because of its vindication of individual freedom. In this sense, autonomy in some degree is universally present in human life even where the choices open to individuals are severely constrained by illiberal social and legal norms. So it will be present to some degree in fascist or communist or political Islamist regimes. There will be many choices that individuals will have to make depending on their position in the regime. Everyone will have to make some decisions about how their lives should go, while elites have to make decisions for those subject to them as well as for themselves.

Some people talk about free will rather than autonomy. I prefer to talk about autonomy because it expresses the potentiality for self-direction or self-determination over a whole life more clearly than free will does. Nevertheless, autonomy is subject to the same sceptical challenge as free will, namely that human beings are never responsible for their "decisions" because these are determined independently of "us" by events in the brain or by a combination of genetic and social factors. In the former case, the conscious belief that we make the decision and are responsible for it must be seen as an idle epiphenomenal reflection of the real determining brain events while, in the latter case, the conscious decision is real, but its content owes nothing to "us" but everything to the genetic and social factors.

I do not intend to get seriously involved in debating these issues in this little book on liberalism. I shall limit myself to a few considerations. With regard to the first suggestion, the claim is that our conscious decisions are made after events in the brain of which we are not aware have already committed us to a course of action. From our perspective as self-conscious beings we are in effect puppets moved by forces operating on us without our knowledge. However, we could never live our lives on the basis of such a belief. We cannot shut off our conscious minds and wait for events in the brain to propel us one way or another. From our point of view as thinking beings we have to believe that what we do is up to us to decide. So, I shall assume that we are autonomous in that sense. In any case, this assumption is not in dispute between liberals, fascists, communists and so on. They all presuppose that human beings are rational agents to some degree who are capable of being responsible for their choices. What is at issue between them is the extent of the ordinary person's capacities and consequently the extent of the rights she should possess to make a whole range of choices for herself.

The second issue does raise questions that are more pressing. I shall consider them in the form of the claim that when we decide to do something on the basis of reasons that we hold are relevant to our decision problem, these reasons are determined in us by a combination of our genetic constitution and our social formation. Given that the consensus view seems to be that our genes at most predispose us to choose certain outcomes, the crucial element in determining the meaningfulness of attributing responsibility to an agent for what she does would seem to lie in the power of the social. So when we decide to do something on the basis of what we think we have most reason to do, it is the social forces we are exposed to acting on our genetic predisposition that is reflected in our apparent choice. It is the values of our society that are reflected in us. We have not chosen these values ourselves after reflection. We have absorbed them and incorporated them unreflectively into our thinking about what is good.

It is certainly the case that the decision-making power of the individual is not exercised in a complete vacuum. A completely arbitrary decision would have no worth. Various forces and considerations inevitably weigh on the decision. Thus my genes and my social formation may push me very strongly in the direction of my acquiring the habit of a daily consumption of alcohol. But I still have to choose to do this. I have to buy the bottles and open them every day. In the normal case, if I become convinced that this habit is ruining my health, I can decide efficaciously to reduce or eliminate the habit. That decision will have been arrived at through the influence of other factors such as my doctor's advice, my family's concerns and health campaigns. But they have to be filtered through my evaluation of their weight relative to the pleasures of drinking and have to culminate in a decision to do one thing or another. The decision-making power is a power to evaluate the factors bearing on a person's appropriate response to the situation in which he finds himself and to come to a decision. He, then, has the capacity to execute his decision through the exercise of his will. The belief in the capacity of human beings for autonomy is just the belief that it is reasonable to attribute to them the capacity, and indeed the necessity, of coming to a decision as to what they should do, given the various forces impinging on them and their genetic disposition, and to hold them responsible for that decision.

However, one suggestion is that I am lacking in autonomy if, for example, I unreflectively acquire and continue the habit of regularly drinking alcohol from the patterns of behaviour of those with whom I associate. I just learn to do what they do and come to enjoy doing it. Many of our "choices" may involve a similar lack of reflective evaluation of the beliefs and values of our society. But unless issues of coercion or manipulation arise, what we do in such an unreflective manner is still imputable to us. Possessing the capacity for reflective evaluation, we could have questioned the expectations of others that led us relatively unthinkingly to do what we did – to go to university, to pursue a legal career, to get married, to vote for the communist party. That we did not, does not mean that we are not responsible for those actions of ours. It does mean, however, that we did not take as much care as we could have done to evaluate our options. Perhaps taking that care we would still have arrived at the same decisions. But we would have exercised a greater degree of autonomy in our lives. We would have taken a greater degree of responsibility for how we want our lives to develop. A liberal society offers its members the opportunity to take that degree of responsibility in the major spheres of life discussed in Part I. It cannot, of course, require its members to take advantage of the opportunities that it offers. It cannot prevent them from unthinkingly following the way of life of their parents, their culture or their contemporaries. But it must promote a culture in which individuals are expected to be aware that it is up to them to decide what to believe and how to live (within the standard constraints) and not authorities such as their parents or their religious or cultural leaders. Such persons are, no doubt, to be respected and listened to, perhaps agreed with but not obeyed, once the individual has become an independent person.

A liberal society offers its members the opportunity to exercise autonomy at two levels that are not present at all or present to a lesser degree in illiberal societies. It must also promote the culture of autonomy at these levels among its members. The first level is autonomy in the major spheres of life. The individual is free to decide for herself her partner, her occupation, her associations and her movements. She may decide not to exercise her rights in these matters other than to allow her parents to make the decisions for her. Or she may decide to live her life on an Australian beach enjoying the sun, the sea and the men. Autonomy in these spheres does not require of the person that she live a life of cumulative achievement but that she takes responsibility for what she does. The first level of autonomy, however, is compatible with a person's choices being the unconsidered reflection of the beliefs and values with which she has learnt, in the first place, to make decisions about what is good and bad. So, she may make her own choices about first level options but only in accordance with the beliefs and values through which she has been formed.

The second level of autonomy covers the sphere of beliefs. A liberal society gives its members the opportunity to decide for themselves what to believe about how the world works and what is good and bad. As I have said before, this does not mean that some beliefs are not much better than others and that people should not pay special respect to the beliefs of those who are generally acknowledged to be experts in a field. Autonomy in the sphere of beliefs does not require the non-astrophysicist to take a view on the truth about black holes. But it does require him to take a view on the values which inform his first level decisions. This does not mean that the person who ignores the opportunity liberalism offers for the reflective evaluation of values is to be "forced" to do so. He may unreflectively identify with the beliefs of his culture or may endorse them after reflection. But a liberal society must promote the culture of second level autonomy and must encourage its members to think in liberal terms. Of course, people formed in a liberal society will begin by thinking in liberal terms. Yet, the culture of second level autonomy will invite them to put liberalism itself to the challenge. A liberal society must constantly expose itself to dissenting voices.

Second level autonomy supposes that it is possible to engage in reflective evaluation about values – that it is possible for instance to give reasons for thinking that one way of socio-political life is better than another and thus that liberalism may or may not be better than communism. At one time many people believed that discussion of values was a waste of time. Fortunately, this is no longer the case. Were it true that rational discussion of values is impossible, then a conservative attitude would seem to be the only viable position. Some set of common values is necessary to maintain the unity of a political society, so one should embrace whatever is the dominant view. Even that judgement supposes that maintaining the existing way of doing things is better than adopting a change that has no point but to put some other elite in power.

Before leaving this section on what autonomy is, I should emphasize that it is not just the quantity of options a person has that matters for determining the degree of that person's autonomy but more importantly their nature and quality. Thus, in the consumers' paradise that is modern capitalism one is faced with choices between a vast array of slightly different consumer goods – innumerable toothpastes, medicines, drinks, cheeses and so on. But having all these choices in respect of food and drink, hygiene and health products would not compensate for the absence of freedom in really important spheres of one's life, such as one's sexual partner, one's religion, one's occupation or one's associates. To say this is not intended to rubbish consumer choice but merely to state that there are more important aspects of life than the choice of one's toothpaste. In general, the more important a sphere is in a person's life, the more important is the question of who is to control the individual's life in that sphere. Should it be the individual adult or some authority that claims to know better than the individual herself how she should live?

Finally, a person's options may be limited in other ways than by illiberal social and legal norms and unreflective normative behaviour. It may be limited by natural causes or by the actions of others. The captain of a ship caught in a violent storm is faced with the decision to jettison his valuable cargo to save the ship and its crew. One may say that the captain had no choice but to jettison the cargo. However, that just means that the decision to jettison the cargo was a no brainer. In another scenario a gunman may draw a gun and say, "your money or your life" (or more strictly, "your money or your life and your money"). Your choice is between handing over your money and trying to disarm the gunman. Again, most probably a no brainer. But here the gunman is wrongly limiting your options. What you are morally entitled to is to enjoy your money and your life without having to defend them. In the former case, it is nature not human beings that is doing the limiting. In both cases, your choice situation is suddenly altered and restricted in a way which limits the degree to which you can be in control of your life. The captain can no longer possess his ship and his cargo without running the risk of losing everything, while the traveller similarly cannot enjoy his life and his money without endangering both of them.

A person's options may also be limited by mental problems from which he suffers. He may be terrified of flying, of open spaces, of speaking in public or indeed of taking decisions. His fear is such that these are not options for him. The fears may be the result of appalling experiences in his past or they may just be the result of a too vivid imagination. In either case the fears cripple him because they prevent him from making an evaluation of his possibilities that is available to the normal human being. By learning to control or overcome his fears he can expand the area of his life that he can take responsibility for through his evaluative capacities and will-power.

THE VALUE OF FREEDOM

Some people think that negative freedom is a value in itself. Indeed, Berlin in his famous essay must treat it as such a value since he distinguishes negative from positive freedom and cautions us against the use of the latter idea. The idea that negative freedom is valuable in itself is one of the sources of libertarianism. Of course, one has first to restrict everyone's negative freedom by the requirement not to invade another's freedom by the exercise of force or fraud. But this can and should be presented as a necessary expression of a regime of equal negative freedom. A state may be held to be also necessary for the maintenance of this regime, but beyond that any interference with a person's negative freedom by other individuals or the state will be an unacceptable violation of a fundamental value. So, on the basis of the inherent value in negative freedom, we can justify only the libertarian minimum state.

However, it is difficult to see what value inheres in negative freedom if we detach it from the positive moment in which the negatively free person determines her own will by choosing something and executing her decision. In itself, negative freedom is the moment in which no one is closing off an option for me. So I can choose to do that thing. Having options and in particular having a range of valuable options is decidedly a good. But it is surely only a good because it enables me to choose among the options I have and hence determine my own future. Suppose that I suffered very badly from an inability to make any but the most trivial decisions about my life. I could decide when to get up in the morning and whether to have coffee or tea for breakfast. But I was quite unable to choose among possible job opportunities, associates or sexual partners. Having to make choices in these matters paralysed me with fear of making the wrong ones and thus of ruining my life. So, I make none and ruin my life anyway. Having the options in this case was detrimental to me. The conclusion would seem to be that having the options is valuable only insofar as it enables people to take control of their lives. If they do not possess this capacity, the freedom would not be valuable for them.

The answer to the question: why should we value negative freedom? must surely be because it is generally better to be in control of one's own will than to be subject to the will of another. The value of negative freedom lies in its necessity for the exercise of autonomy, and autonomy is at least a fundamental human value. This claim applies in the first instance to adults and is a presumption only. Some adults may have little capacity for autonomy because of their limited understanding of how the natural and social worlds work. Such people are natural dependents and need to be under the care of responsible adults. Others have the intellectual capacity to enjoy a high degree of autonomy but because of deficiencies of character and judgement have a strong tendency to make a mess of their lives. They might be better off if others made decisions for them.

Autonomy, in some degree, is the essential human mode of being in the world. It is the ability to reflect on one's options and evaluate them through the medium of reasons and to control one's actions by one's choices. The development and exercise of this ability is absolutely necessary for the existence of adults who can govern themselves by the prudential and ethical prescriptions of any human regime whatsoever, whether liberal or illiberal. The latter may be paternalists like Plato's philosophers, or religious leaders, or communist party elites, or they may be small-scale societies held together by an unreflective attachment to tribal customs. All such regimes must develop in their members the ability to apprehend the meaning and value of the rules they prescribe for living well and acting ethically and the ability to apply those rules to their lives. In other words, an illiberal regime cannot but recognize the importance for itself of its members' self-regulation and thus the importance of autonomy in some degree. To deny this would be to forego the most effective means of exercising its rule and to abandon any claim to be a community of human beings aimed at satisfying its members' fundamental interests. Instead of being the source of rules, claimed to be in the best interests of its members, which it teaches the members to impose on themselves, the regime would have to rely entirely on brute force. In this sense, then, such regimes must rule through the human capacity for autonomy and hence must attach a value to it in itself as an essential dimension of human life. Of course, an illiberal regime necessarily limits the exercise of this capacity to a greater degree than a liberal one. While it must depend on its subjects' capacity for autonomy up to a point, it must discourage them from its exercise in reflectively evaluating the worth of the rules and values which it requires them to follow.

Since autonomy is a matter of degree, it is possible that the capacity for autonomy is distributed among human beings in a very uneven manner. It is possible that a few people possess the capacity to a high degree and the rest to varying but much lower degrees. Such a distribution of the capacity could be the basis for a Platonic type regime in which a small intellectual elite rule with the help of an auxiliary class of law-enforcers over a class of workers. The fact that autonomy is a fundamental human value does not lead directly to the vindication of liberalism. To get to a liberal society, one would have to claim that either everyone possesses the capacity to an equal degree or that everyone possesses a threshold level of the capacity that entitles them to enjoy the full liberal rights. The discussion of this issue would take us from the account of the meaning and value of freedom to that of equality, which is the subject of the next chapter.

Does the rejection of the claim that negative freedom is a value in itself and is valuable only as the condition of autonomy destroy the case for libertarianism? Not obviously. Why should the libertarian not agree with the second claim? Indeed, this is the position that can be attributed to Robert Nozick, a noted 20th-century libertarian, whose views I will discuss in Part III.

FURTHER READING

The main essays in this field can be found in Miller (1991). A clear introduction to the idea of freedom is Swift (2001).

On autonomy, see the chapter in Raz (1986); G. Dworkin (1990); also Sneddon (2013) and R. Young (2017). Gray (2015) tries to persuade us that we are only puppets while Baggini (2015) is a clear defence of our free will.

NOTES

1. The essay can be found in Berlin (1969).
2. See the essay by MacCallum in Miller (1991).
3. Locke (1964) 2nd Treatise, para 57.
4. Rousseau (1964) p.64.

THE EQUALITY OF THE PARTICIPANTS

EQUALITY OF STATUS

The meaning of the concept of equality is not a problem. To apply the term there must be at least two different entities that in some respect are the same. If a+b equals c+d, then a and b must add up to the same number as c and d. Jones and Smith may be equal in some respect. They may be the same height or weight or whatever. In a liberal society, the members are standardly claimed to relate to each other as equals. What is this relationship of equality? Insofar as to be a member of a liberal society is to enjoy the rights described in Part I, then the members' equality consists in the first instance in an equality of rights in those spheres of life governed by liberal practices. Since in these spheres each person is entitled to decide for herself what to believe and how to live (within the standard constraints), the members may be said to enjoy an equal status in the society. Since each is, in principle, in charge of her own life, no one should be subject to the will of another. These rights determine the basic structure of society as this is constructed through the society's laws and institutions. Through their operation the equality of the members is given reality.

A distinction has been drawn in the contemporary philosophical literature on equality between equality as a distributive principle and equality as a social and political ideal. The former involves the idea of distributing some stuff e.g. money or well-being so that people have equal amounts of it. This is the interpretation of liberalism that I call egalitarian liberalism and discuss in the next section. Equality as a social and political ideal is not about distributing some stuff but about securing mutual respect between citizens who see themselves as equals. This is what I call equality of status. It excludes the existence of all hierarchical relations between citizens in regard to their status as citizens, whether formal or informal. However poor a citizen is, no one is expected to doff their cap to another, pull their forelock, stand aside to give the other precedence because the other is deemed to be a superior. Such signs of social inferiority and superiority involve, from the point of view of the ideal of equality of status, demeaning relations that must be expunged from the society. It may well be that it is difficult to realize this ideal of an equality of status in a society where there exist great inequalities of condition. This issue will be an important concern in my subsequent account of liberalism. Nevertheless, what is fundamental to the ideal is not distributive equality but the equal possession of basic liberal rights through which each person is in a position to be master of her own life and subject to no one. As Rousseau did not quite put it: each is independent of the others and dependent only on the community through which everyone acquires their rights.[1]

This equality of status does not mean that associations and institutions in which some members are subject to the authority of others are unacceptable. Some associations enjoying the liberal right of free association have an authoritarian structure. By this I mean not only that the organization is governed by an elite group but also that new leaders are not chosen by the members but appointed by existing ones. Many religious organizations, such as the Catholic and Anglican Churches, are like this but so also are universities and innumerable other associations. There is nothing incompatible with liberal rights in such arrangements provided that the right of members to leave the association, if they so wish, is preserved. So, even if they became members through no choice of their own but only through their parents making them members, and provided they can leave on reasonable terms, their liberal rights will not have been violated. Unreasonable terms consist in persecution and harassment making it impossible for the leaver to live a normal life.

Similarly, accepting an offer of paid employment standardly involves subjecting oneself to some degree to the direction of those in authority in the business. But it would be incompatible with a person's status as an equal if he were forced by his economic circumstances to agree to a contract that enslaves him to his employer. The law, indeed, goes much further than this in protecting a potential paid employee from onerous and exploitative contracts as described in the relevant sections of Part I. However, the subject of the economic and social conditions that everyone must enjoy, if his status as an equal is to be achieved, is of great importance and I shall return to it later.

Voluntary associations may, of course, have a democratic organizational structure. The members may appoint the leaders or, if small enough, may exercise the authority of the association together. But in a liberal society no one should be compelled to join such an association or be unable to leave. Hence, it will still be up to the individual to decide whether to join an association that involves pooling his decision-making rights with others or to continue to do so. If so, the primacy of individual decision-making and individual responsibility will be preserved.

If the political society is democratic as well as liberal, then the members have an opportunity together to reject their leaders and appoint new ones. But an individual member cannot decide that he will not pay his taxes or obey a particular law because, although a member will have the right in a liberal society to emigrate to another society if there is one that will accept him, he cannot decide to leave the political association while remaining in its territory. Political association is the sphere of collective and not individual action. We are all in it together in the sense that whatever the type of political regime, the decision of its political authorities is binding on everyone in the territory. The only choice the members have, apart from leaving the territory if they can, is to replace the regime with another – a choice that, in potentially involving rebellion, carries with it severe dangers. As a sphere of collective action the liberal idea of individual decision-making cannot apply. The hierarchies of authority in the political realm, then, cannot be escaped unless the whole population could exercise together the authority of the collective through constant referenda. However, such hierarchies can be made accountable to the people through democratic institutions, in which the people enjoy equal political rights, and through the rule of law.

There will be in a liberal society, besides the hierarchies of authority in voluntary associations and the non-voluntary hierarchies of politics, informal hierarchies of excellence that will be found in all activities: in sport, thinking, business, technology, art, politics, morals and so on. Special respect and rewards for such excellences are in no sense in conflict with the spirit or practice of liberalism. What would be incompatible with liberal equality of status would be the granting to such superior performers privileges such as special voting rights or greater freedoms in regard to speech, association, movement and economy than were possessed by the ordinary citizen. John Locke, in a famous passage, expresses this distinction between a fundamental equality of status enjoyed by all men and the inequalities they are subject to that are nevertheless compatible with it thus:

> [t]hough I have said that all men by nature are equal, I cannot be supposed to understand all sorts of equality; age or virtue may give men a just precedency; excellency of parts and merit may place others above the common level; birth may subject some and alliance and benefits others to pay an observance to those to whom nature, gratitude or other respects may have made it due; and yet all this consists with the equality which all men are in, in respect of jurisdiction or dominion one over another, which was the equality I there spoke of, as proper to the business in hand, being that equal right that every man has to his natural freedom without being subject to the will or authority of any other man.[2]

The equal status enjoyed by members of a liberal and democratic society is to be contrasted with the position of individuals in societies organized hierarchically into ranks. Historically, the latter have been monarchies supported by a military class of nobles and a priestly class promoting a belief system that endorses the established order in which the privileged classes rule over the workers. In the 20th century the opposition to the equality of liberal-democratic society has been led by fascist and communist states in which a monopoly of political and ideological power is held by the leaders of a party claiming to have a unique understanding of the interests of the people. The fascist states openly deride the rights beloved of liberals that protect the individual's freedom and substitute for the rule of law the rule of the party and its officials who are supposed to embody the collective interest. The communist states, while their practice is identical to the fascists, nevertheless issue constitutions that claim to guarantee the liberal rights of its citizens. But these rights have to be exercised in the interests of the workers as interpreted by the party. Since the party's interests are supposed to be identical to the interests of the workers, the party may override the rights whenever it thinks its interests require it.

One-party states, in effect, divide the population into a ruling class of party officials on the one hand and their subjects on the other. There are now, however, de facto one-party states that are called managed or illiberal democracies. Russia under Putin is the model of such a state. The forms of democratic institutions and procedures, liberal rights and the rule of law are preserved, but one party has succeeded in capturing the legal institutions and the media which enables it to manipulate public opinion, use the law to obstruct its opponents and together with outright fraud and thuggery to maintain itself in power.

EGALITARIAN LIBERALISM

The equality of status of members of a liberal society is not the only way liberal equality may be conceived. However, in order to understand these other conceptions, it is necessary first to seek an answer to the question of why the members should be committed to a sense of their fundamental moral equality. The problem of why we should attach a fundamental value to the equality of the members was seen to arise in the discussion of the value of freedom. If, as I argued in that discussion, the value of negative freedom lies in its making possible the autonomy of the individual and autonomy is a matter of degree, some people having a greater capacity for autonomy than others, then why should this inequality of autonomy not be reflected in the social and political organization of society? We could have special votes and legal privileges regarding speech for the more autonomous, while the less autonomous might be subject to restrictions of various kinds on their freedom of speech, movement, association and sexual partners.

One move in defence of a fundamental equality of rights and status for the members is to claim that, even if it is true that autonomy comes in degrees and some people have a greater capacity for autonomy than others, nevertheless, we are all equally morally worthy beings and our fundamental interests should count equally. However, this claim can be accepted while denying that it must conclude in a strongly egalitarian society. For it is compatible with what I call Platonism – the conception of a just society as one divided into ranks determined by people's level of understanding of the good for human beings. While the less wise are subjected to those with greater understanding, the fundamental interests of each class in living a good human life will be best satisfied by such a hierarchical order. This conception of a fundamental moral equality of members of a political society may be said to be necessary for understanding it as a community in the first place. The members of such a community must be able to recognize each other as equally ends – that is to say not just as means to the achievement of some goal. As ends, their fundamental interests must count equally in the determination of a just basic structure of rights and duties for the society. Yet, as the Platonist argument shows, such a moral equality is compatible with a hierarchy of ranks.

To get from fundamental moral equality to egalitarian liberalism or indeed to any kind of liberalism, we need additional arguments. One such argument consists in an appeal to a threshold level of attainment of autonomy that justifies the granting of the same liberal rights to everyone. Everybody is capable of passing the threshold and hence is entitled to the liberal rights. Although beyond the threshold there exist inequalities in people's capacity for autonomy, these are held to be irrelevant to the distribution of rights. In effect, the egalitarian liberal assumes that the inequalities are irrelevant because of the kind of ethical claim he makes about the inherent worth of individuals. Passing the threshold activates so to speak a claim that an autonomous being can make to be treated as a being of absolute worth. Such beings are necessarily of equal worth. This worth gets transferred to a person's autonomous choices. Hence, the fundamental interests of each person consists in being able to realize his autonomous choices. Since each person has an equal claim in this regard, a just society will be one which recognizes this equality in some way. The choice here is roughly between trying to secure an equality of outcome by adjusting people's resources to give them an equal chance of realizing their ends, or trying to make sure that people possess the same amount of resources to start with so they have to adjust their choice of ends to their fair share of resources. Either way, this conception of a just liberal society involves a much more substantial equality than is present in the idea of an equality of status. It involves a presumption that there should be an equal distribution of the means to autonomous individuals' well-being. I shall call this type of conception of an equal freedom egalitarian liberalism. It contrasts with the libertarian liberalism referred to in the previous chapter.

I should mention at this point that I shall be discussing in Part III two prominent recent theories of broadly egalitarian liberal sympathy that start with the presumption of an equal distribution of the means to well-being but nevertheless justify departures from this initial equality. One is the theory of John Rawls. His theory affirms the initial justice of an equal distribution of what he calls primary social goods: liberties, opportunities, income, wealth and the sources of self-respect. But he believes, roughly, that departures from such an initial equality that maximize the long-run amount possessed by the worst-off group are justified. The other theory is standardly called luck egalitarianism and its most prominent advocate was Ronald Dworkin. Luck egalitarianism allows inequalities in the command of resources that are attributable to people's free choices but disallows inequalities that can be attributed to the forces of brute luck. The basic idea of this theory is that no one should be better or worse off than another in terms of her command of resources due to circumstances over which she has no control such as her natural talents or other forms of brute luck. However, becoming better off, through one's free choice to work hard and save and invest, than another with the same abilities who chooses to spend her days on the beach, is acceptable.

Egalitarian liberalism is standardly justified on the grounds of the inherent and equal worth of autonomous individuals. Some people think that egalitarianism rests on the belief that equality is a value in itself that a liberal society necessarily endorses. That the relation of equality might be considered a value in itself, however, is an absurdity. It would mean claiming that there is something inherently valuable in the fact that some or all people are the same in some respect e.g. that they are the same height or weight or have the same colour hair. Temkin, indeed, accepts this implication. He says that in a society in which everyone is blind except for one person, the equality that would result from the blinding of that person would count as a good in itself, although no doubt overridden by the evils involved in the blinding.[3] In fact, if the value inheres in nothing but the equality relation, it will exist in equal relations between non-human things also. So, it is inherently a good thing that two trees are the same height. All this is nonsense. The inherent value of equality, if it exists, must identify a relation between human beings. But then it is fairly obvious that, if we are attributing an inherent value to an equal relation between human beings, it must be because the human beings are of inherent value in themselves. So, we return to what I call the standard version of the ground of egalitarian liberalism.

This standard version has been, recently, the often unacknowledged basis for the popularity of egalitarian liberalism in the political theory departments of English-speaking academies. It is, nevertheless, a no more acceptable version of liberalism than the libertarian one. I shall be exploring the grounds for rejecting these theories in Part III in the form of the developed ideas of their most prominent advocates. If one is an adherent of libertarianism or egalitarianism, this will profoundly affect one's view of the proper bounds of liberal economic freedom. The libertarian, on the one hand, is strongly moved to reject any government limitations on the freedom of economic actors designed to protect people's interests from anything other than the exercise of force, fraud and breach of contract. The egalitarian, on the other, wants the government to create a world in which economic and social conditions and/or outcomes are roughly the same for all. Traditionally, economic freedom has been and largely still is the main field of differentiation of the two extreme versions of liberalism. However, more recently, the egalitarian doctrine has come to have propound effects on the debates about cultural identity and values. Libertarians, naturally, believe that this dimension of life should be governed by individual choice, and cultures should be left to flourish or die according to the support they can obtain on the basis of the principle of individual choice. Some egalitarians have come to extend their demands for equality of conditions and/or outcomes to the enjoyment by persons of their cultural identity and values. I will be discussing these claims in the next two sections. The issues between these versions of liberalism also affects their respective positions on aspects of free speech. The egalitarian will seek to ensure that the opportunities for participation in free speech are as much as possible the same for all while the libertarian thinks that mere possession of equal formal rights to speak will be sufficient to satisfy everyone's legitimate claims.

It might be thought that something like egalitarian liberalism follows from the liberal commitment to an equality of status. The status of a member of liberal society as an equal depends in the first place on her possession of all the liberal rights. But suppose that she was born into a destitute family that only survived through scavenging from day to day. She received no education and had no opportunities to improve her condition other than by prostitution or drug-trafficking. Since the one is degrading and the other illegal, they cannot count as acceptable options through which to develop her powers of autonomy. Her only option is in effect scavenging. This is not an occupation for someone who is supposed to enjoy an equality of status with reasonably paid workers by hand and brain, and it does not provide her with a good reason to respect their equal rights. It is obvious that her rights, which should enable her to exercise her powers of autonomy in taking control of her life, have little value for her. They will have value only for those people who have received a certain level of education and have access to a certain level of resources, which give them some valuable options for running their lives, and the understanding of the world to choose intelligently among them. That level cannot be specified with any certainty since it will depend on the nature and wealth of the society. But that is not the issue under discussion here. The question is whether the distribution of resources or opportunities must be equal for the members to be said to enjoy an equality of status. The wealthy and the better endowed and better connected no doubt have better opportunities than those who are poorer in these respects. But does that give them a higher status in regard to the fundamentals of citizenship? Both the richer and the poorer have the same rights, and, in that sense, they have the same status. So, the issue would seem to have to depend on whether the poorer had sufficient resources and opportunities to put them in control of their own lives. Only if the greater resources of wealth and talent of the richer ipso facto enabled them to control the lives of those less well-endowed would there be a strong case for an equality of resources grounded in the demands of an equality of status. Such dependency of the poor on the rich is possible, but it clearly does not follow from merely being better off than another. One has to attend, then, not to inequality per se but to areas of dependency in liberal society and take measures to prevent them from occurring. This view of an appropriate distribution of resources and opportunities is sometimes called sufficientism: everyone must have access to a sufficient level of resources and options to be able to make valuable choices in running his own life.

In Part III these ideas of what sort of equality is required by liberalism will be explored further in the form of the main comprehensive theories of liberalism.

EQUALITY AND FEMINISM

The rights of members of a liberal society are rights of individual human beings arising from their individual nature as capable, first, of taking responsibility for their individual lives and, second, of cooperating with the other members in exercising collective responsibility for how their society is run. The early feminist movement in the 19th century was concerned primarily with acquiring for women the same rights over their own lives as the male members of their society already possessed. In fighting for equal rights for women, the movement had to overcome deeply embedded patriarchal attitudes which involved seeing women as essentially dependent beings in need of direction and support by fathers and husbands. The standard patriarchal view was that women were by nature governed by their emotions rather than by reason. Aristotle – a Platonist in his political thinking except in regard to women – allowed that women were capable of following a rational argument, as indeed natural slaves were, and also accepted that they possessed a deliberative faculty. But he held that it was without authority because it was dominated by their passions. As the rational element is superior to the passionate and should rule the passions, so he claimed "the male is by nature superior and the female inferior".[4] So, to claim equality with men in a liberal society, the feminists had to argue that if women appeared more emotional and less rational than men, it was not because they were essentially inferior to men in these respects but because they were denied the education and mental discipline that enabled men to rationalize their domination of them.

Women in western states gained the formal rights to run their own lives in the course of the 19th and 20th centuries. But rights to own and control property, to the freedoms of speech, association and movement were insufficient for this purpose for middle and upper class women, who constituted the backbone of the liberal feminist movement, without their access to a higher education and to a professional career. Working class women had been working in domestic or factory production without enjoying the liberal rights for a long time, but for most women in the feminist movement this was hardly the life options they desired. So, the goal of liberal feminism was and is not simply to have the same rights as men but to have, broadly, the same range of options and to receive equal pay for equal work. The gender gap in pay and in opportunities, especially at the higher levels in most occupations, is still a matter of serious concern for such feminists.

Liberal feminism seeks equal rights, status and opportunities for women with men. Part of the problem in securing the latter is thought to lie in the different natures and corresponding cultures of men and women at work as well as to the continuation of traditional distinctions between male and female roles in the family. Women continue to spend more time caring for the family's children and doing the housework than men in western liberal societies even though men have come a long way in these respects. In the workplace, men are said to be more ambitious, aggressive and competitive while women have more caring and cooperative attitudes. So, women are reluctant to engage in the fight for the top jobs.

One radical way of attempting to deal with this problem has been to treat the whole question of women's equality as a problem in identity politics. Identity politics is so-called because it involves seeing people's different interests, which a polity must seek to harmonize, as arising from their different cultural identities. This form of feminism has come to be known as difference feminism. Women and men have different natures. These natures are expressed in different ways of living together or different cultures. Women are said to constitute a minority culture, not in terms of gross numbers of course but in terms of the status of their culture. Because of this inferior status their culture is discriminated against by the dominant male culture. The two cultures are identified in very traditional terms. Women's identity is oriented towards their emotions, feelings and bodily senses and expresses itself in an ethics of care and love. Men's identity is oriented towards rationality, abstraction and impersonality. It is expressed in systems of law and rights. Thus, modern state law and the notion of the sovereign state are represented as the articulation of a male point of view which "constructs the legal subject as a rational individual in control of its cognitive capacities, inhabiting a public sphere and abstracted from affective ties".[5] The rights guaranteed in that law protect individual choices over goods and activities, which is a typical male idea. Women's ethical concerns are realized in relationships and through collective goods. These ideas are, remarkably, the staple stuff of patriarchal attitudes. If this is indeed how women are, then since by the nature of the entities reason must govern (but not suppress) emotion, men must govern women.

Of course, the difference feminists reach a different conclusion. First of all, women should not be identified as primarily individuals possessing the features of individuality, rationality and autonomy. This is what men are. Women are caring and cooperative beings whose value arises from their participation in groups that express these attitudes. Second, to treat women equally with men now ceases to be a matter of bestowing men's rights on women but becomes a question of treating women's culture equally with that of men's. The immediate trouble with this proposal is that the two cultures are incompatible as features of one system that unites all persons subject to it. You cannot have a society whose basic structure consists of liberal individualist forms of interaction and at the same time one whose basic structure is anti-liberal. It must be admitted that the difference feminists are very vague about what forms of interaction would characterize a society based on difference feminist norms. But I presume that in view of their emphasis on caring and cooperation, these norms would aspire to be a kind of socialism. In that case, either the liberal-individualist norms must dominate the socialist ones or conversely. Yet, that stand-off supposes that we cannot but envisage a society as a single unified system of norms or rather aspiring to that condition. From that point of view, any residual incoherence in a society's set of norms would count as a defect in them that requires attention and remedy. But this is not what they have in mind. Their proposal is that we should think of the shared public space of a society, not as requiring everyone's commitment to the same norms but as a place in which representatives of different cultures can reach ad hoc settlements. What these would be like cannot be determined in advance except that, as they will not be based on any common principles, they will be forms of modus vivendi resulting from the relative power of the negotiators. There is little to be said for such a scheme from an ethical point of view.

Difference feminism is not a form of liberalism. Indeed, there is an incoherence at its base. It rejects the liberal conception of the value of the individual as arising from her capacity to take responsibility for her own life and so must reject the claim to equality that is derived from that conception. Yet, it still demands an equality of respect for women's culture which, if you remove the liberal base for such an equality, rests on nothing whatsoever. There is no reason to give equal respect to different cultures as such when some are murderous gangs of warriors, such as the Vikings, one of whose objects was to rob, rape and kill their neighbours, while many others are organized for the domination and exploitation of their women and other workers. You would have to show that a culture is worthy of respect and to do so by appealing to the values it expresses. However, the issues raised by the claim of the difference feminists to an equality of respect for women's culture are of more general significance which I will deal with in the next section on equality and multi-culturalism.

Before leaving the ideas of the difference feminists on women's nature, I would make the following points. Even if we accept their idea of a significant difference between male and female natures, this must be a difference in the degree to which the 'masculine' and 'feminine' elements in human nature are combined in particular individuals. It is surely absurd and wholly derogatory to suppose that women are without the capacity for rationality and abstraction and have no interest in law, rights or entitlements. Equally absurd would be to suppose that men have no emotions or feelings, do not care for, or love, others and have no concern for collective goods.

Of course, it has to be recognized that these terms – the masculine and the feminine – are to some degree social constructs that can be modified. Some writers even take the view that they are wholly social constructs and that there are no essential natures of men and women. This is, broadly, the view of the post-modern feminists who are now quite prominent. But it is completely self-defeating to try to base a form of feminism on such a radical idea. For, if at bottom there is no masculine or feminine, then there is no 'woman' to whom any injustice is being done by a particular social construction of the feminine.

Let us assume, then, that there is a natural difference between the sexes and that it consists in a different balance between the emotional and rational capacities of individuals. Then, the issue is whether women in respect of their rational and autonomous capacities have an interest in rights and law. Similarly, for men, the issue is whether in respect of their emotional nature they have an interest in personal relationships and collective goods. Frankly, it is insulting to the intelligence of any normal person to be expected to answer these questions. Nevertheless, we still have to raise the issue of whether within the system of liberal rights that protects individuals' autonomy and equality, the emotional needs and caring ethical dispositions of both men and women can be satisfied.

In the first place, individual liberty rights do not obviously exclude personal relationships of love and friendship unless we treat any suggestion for developing a close relation as an assault on the other person's liberty. Otherwise, the framework of rights within which such relationships must be carried on merely sets legal limits to the oppression and exploitation that is possible within them. In the second place, there are many professions in which care for others should be a central concern, such as the medical, teaching and social work professions together with the huge range of charitable organizations. In the third place, the ethics of concern has already captured the public sphere in the form of welfare liberalism. The attempt to expand this ethic in the public sphere to all activities by eliminating individual liberty rights is the project of collectivist socialism on the

Soviet model. From a liberal point of view, this is the most stupid political enterprise to which human beings have committed themselves. It is true that the collectivized welfare of the liberal welfare state is far removed from the ethics of personal relations endorsed by the difference feminists, yet together with the public sphere in general it constitutes a collective good which these feminists, rather absurdly, believe that 'masculinity' rejects.

Thus, there are plenty of reasons for thinking that the 'masculine' and 'feminine' interests of both men and women have reasonable scope for satisfaction in a liberal society. At the same time, that answer does not deal with the question of whether the opportunities for women in career advancement throughout society are sufficiently equal to those of men. Here it may still be necessary to attempt to alter the balance between the masculine and feminine elements in liberal job culture.

It might be appropriate here to discuss the claims of transgender people. I am not thinking of people who have undergone hormonal and surgical treatment to enable them to be reallocated to the sex of their preference but of those who are hormonally and organically members of one sex and yet, subjectively, systematically think of themselves as members of the other. In a liberal society anyone can think of herself as she pleases, but there may be circumstances in which there are good public reasons for overriding her self-classification and requiring her to conform to a supposedly objective one. Furthermore, even though, subjectively, she may think of herself as she pleases, she is not entitled to impose her view of herself on others. She may believe that, although being objectively white and having no black genes in her family, she is, in an important sense for her, essentially black or an Eskimo or a very stable genius. But she cannot demand that everyone else identifies her on the same basis. They may think she is a moron and are entitled to say so.

If transgender self-identifications do not fall into the same category as these hypothetical oddities, it must be on grounds that have some objective basis. In this case it must be because the categories of male and female sex are to a certain degree unstable. This is almost certainly true. Given a clear standard differentiation of male and female individuals, there will be a range of exceptions, such as hermaphrodites, mistaken classifications and hormonal imbalances.

Assuming, then, that there is some objective basis for transgender self-identifications, the question is whether this gives rise to any problems in the distributions of rights? In a liberal society, the bottom line must be that transgender people are entitled to the same rights as anyone else. So, it would be wrong to discriminate against them in employment, housing, health services and so on. However, society is not organized in some respects to accommodate them as with sexually differentiated toilets and changing rooms, men's and women's sporting events and the ubiquitous official forms demanding whether you are male or female. The problem with changing rooms and toilets could be avoided by having only unisex ones. Official forms could add transgender categories. But having only unisex sports events would not be right. In this case and also where advantages have been accorded women through the use of women quotas in employment, the simple binary classification of all human beings is in conflict with the experience of transgender people, and there is no obvious way of resolving the conflict other than by adding new sports categories and employment quotas.

EQUALITY AND MULTI-CULTURALISM

A liberal political society will have a dominant political culture which will, unsurprisingly, be a liberal one. Within that society there may be many sub-groups with their own cultures. Such groups will have a common identity shared by the members. This identity may be based on religion, ethnicity, nationality, gender, sexual orientation, political affiliation, language and innumerable other possible common interests. A liberal society will allow these groups to exist and to promote their beliefs and values within the standard constraints discussed in the relevant sections of Part I. These constraints consist in the requirement not to violate the equal rights of others, not to libel others, not to endanger national security or public safety. The groups' rights of association and speech will be derived from the rights of their individual members. It is because the groups' individual members have rights to associate with whom they please, to believe what they think best and to seek new members and believers that their chosen organized groupings have the same rights. It is likely, then, that a liberal society will be a multi-cultural one in the sense of having within it many different associations with their own sets of beliefs and values, all of which enjoy the liberal freedoms. Indeed, the emergence of liberalism as a distinct idea for a novel form of social organization had probably as much to do with the idea of religious tolerance – the idea of living together at peace in the same political society with people of different religious beliefs – as with the growth in interest in economic freedom on the part of a rising bourgeois class that is the more traditional narrative of Marxist-inclined historians.

This form of multi-culturalism may be called liberal multi-culturalism. It is in no sense a challenge to liberalism but is rather a standard application of it. The form of multi-culturalism that is thought by some people to present a serious challenge to liberalism is one tied to identity politics. As noted in the previous section on difference feminism, identity politics treats a person's fundamental identity and interests as determined by her membership of a cultural group, that is, by the beliefs and values of the group she most strongly identifies herself with. So, a woman may grow up as a Muslim in British society and never question this identity. What it means for her to be a Muslim is determined for her by the beliefs and practices through which her identity as a Muslim has been formed. But it is clear that she could come to doubt aspects of this identity or even the identity as a whole. She might, then, overcome her doubts and re-affirm her commitment to it, modify it in part or reject it altogether. So, her initial, and possible subsequent, identification of herself as a Muslim is compatible with liberal practices of free speech and free association even if the form of life she identifies herself with is profoundly anti-liberal.

Under liberalism her anti-liberal beliefs and practices will be tolerated but not supported or encouraged and not recognized as valid in the educational and ideological institutions of the liberal state. In this sense, one might say that equal respect is not being given to these anti-liberal forms of life where this means that they are not treated as equally valid forms of belief and living as those that broadly endorse the liberal perspective. Since a liberal society congratulates itself on giving equal respect to its members, the inadequacy of liberal toleration in this regard is considered a defect in its practice. This criticism of liberalism is obviously absurd from a liberal perspective since it is a recommendation to a liberal society to commit suicide. It appears to ignore the fact that liberalism constitutes the hegemonic rule unifying the members in one society. So, it cannot, while remaining true to its beliefs that it has a right to rule in this society by determining what is and what is not acceptable, at the same time acknowledge that it has no such right and that anti-liberalism is equally valid with itself.

However, objection to this hegemonic claim of liberalism is precisely what motivates this form of identity-based multi-culturalism. Intellectually, it is grounded in the belief that liberalism is incapable of justifying its right to be considered a superior form of life to anti-liberal alternatives. Yet, this is not just a defect within liberalism but true for all the ideological views or faiths on offer. The conclusion that is reached is that all should be equally respected. William Connolly, a noted theorist of this form of multi-culturalism, has made a brave attempt to show why this would not lead to complete chaos. He contrasts what he calls the shallow pluralism of liberalism with his own deep pluralism. Shallow pluralism arises from liberalism's apparent treatment of different faiths as just a body of beliefs. It can, thus, confine the faith with its truncated identity in a private realm which thereby excludes it from participation in the public-political sphere. What shallow pluralism leaves out of consideration are the lived practices and rituals in which the faith's beliefs are embodied. Deep pluralism by contrast recognizes the faith as a unity of belief and embodied practice and, as a result, apparently must allow the faith in its full particularity to participate in the public-political realm. This recognition of the faith as a valid occupant of the public realm ensures that you must have some way of facing up to its claims other than by merely tolerating them.

What he proposes is a practice of agonistic respect. This is different from liberal tolerance because, under the latter, we do not have to confront the way in which others differ in their beliefs and practices from us. We just let each other be. Under agonistic respect, we make claims on others based on our beliefs and practices, and others are supposed to respond in kind. Initially, we confront each other with our opposed views, each demanding hegemony – suppose I am a Muslim patriarchalist and you are a liberal feminist. But then we are expected to acknowledge that we cannot substantiate our claims to hegemony and must accept that the other's view is to be respected as equally valid with our own. This constitutes the agonizing element in the practice. Subsequently, we are supposed to enter into a negotiation with the other with the aim of arriving at an agreed position.

Given that Connolly envisages a vast array of minorities participating in these negotiated settlements, both the procedures and outcomes are very unclear. Do these negotiated settlements conclude in binding public policies and laws? If not, what political status do they have? If they do, how are the laws and policies supposed to be determined? Do the thousands of groups have rights to be represented in the legislative body? Or are they supposed to operate through traditional liberal-democratic forms and parties? On the whole, Connolly seems committed to the latter. The faith groups would seek to obtain their own representatives through membership of one of the umbrella parties or as a separate party of their own. If the procedures of agonistic respect are widely followed, the resulting public policies produced through the liberal democratic constitution will undoubtedly be different. However, they are not compulsory. They are to be promoted through education and example and otherwise support for them is presumed to be motivated by considerations very similar to those involved in the support of liberalism, namely, fear of persecution and civil strife. Yet, since the results of trying to follow the procedures in reaching negotiated settlements that all members of opposed faiths can accept must be doubtful in the extreme, the chances of their being widely followed seems small, especially when the simplicities of liberal tolerance lie close at hand as an alternative.

WHY SHOULD WE OPT FOR DEEP PLURALISM RATHER THAN LIBERAL TOLERANCE?

Connolly cannot say that it is because deep pluralism is a better hegemonic principle than liberalism or all the others. He would, then, be hoist with his own petard. In any case it is totally unclear whether an organizing principle would emerge from the agonizing chaos. As a result, much of his language describes ways in which people can be attracted to following agonistic respect of their own accord. Yet, he makes implicit appeals to the sovereignty of deep pluralism. First, by proposing that it should be promoted by education and example. Who is to do this promotion? If the state is, that could be justified only if deep pluralism had a right to command the state in this respect. If it is to be done through private establishments, then no such implicit hegemonic claims would be involved. Second, and much more conclusively, he acknowledges that should a hegemony-seeking faith resort to unprovoked violence in support of its aims, then you may want (!) to call in the police or military to protect you and suppress the aggressors. This presupposes the existence of a state with a right to use violence according to some rule. So, some hegemonic principle is involved. Presumably, it should be deep pluralism, although it could be shallow liberalism. Either way the appeal to state forces to impose such a rule would be unjustified in terms of deep pluralism's own underlying intellectual suppositions.

Deep pluralism is unsustainable as the hegemonic principle of an independent political society. Without such a status and without relying, disingenuously, on the order provided by a liberal state, it would be a recipe for chaos. Some people may wish, nevertheless, to follow its practices within a liberal society. They would be tolerated. However, deep pluralism suffers from other defects besides a deep incoherence. The first is the very contrast between it and shallow pluralism. Liberalism is shallow, it is claimed, because it limits the understanding of faiths to a core of beliefs ignoring their embodiment in practices and rituals. Thereby, it is able to confine the faith to a private realm in which it can be ignored politically. Both these claims are false. Liberalism tolerates both the beliefs and practices of a faith provided their adherents do not engage in violence or advocate it in circumstances in which criminal acts are likely to be committed. You cannot tolerate the practices of a faith unless you recognize them. Furthermore, in what sense does liberalism exclude beliefs and practices of faiths from the public realm? The private realm is defined by a set of freedom rights which allow you to think and live as you please subject to the standard limits. But these rights don't forbid you to participate in the public realm on the basis of your beliefs and values. There is nothing within liberalism which forbids the formation of Christian political parties or Muslim ones. What liberalism objects to are policies from whatever source that would violate people's equal rights. If these rights are written into a constitution, then the adoption of policies violating them would be unconstitutional. But under liberal free speech practices you could still advocate these policies in the public realm and you can always advocate changing the constitution. In a vibrant liberal democracy, the advocacy of illiberal policies will not get you very far. But this is quite different from saying that such beliefs are excluded from the public realm. What characterizes the public realm is that laws and policies adopted in due constitutional form are binding on everyone. In the private realm, what I believe or how I live is no business of anyone else unless they are freely associated with me.

Another problem with deep pluralism is the question of what the subject of negotiation between opposed faiths is supposed to be. It is not, one would think, about who has the better reasons for believing in their different faiths. Deep pluralism is founded on the rejection of this possibility. So, it would have to be a compromise over their respective practices. The liberal feminist would have to accept some degree of subordination in exchange for an element of equality elsewhere. How profoundly dispiriting! Anyway, how are such agreements to be made binding on all women or all patriarchalists? If they are not binding, then they are merely private agreements between a few parties, to which liberalism could have no objection.

The root of the trouble with this form of multi-culturalism is its claim that no set of beliefs about the right or the best hegemonic principle can be justified. So all forms of living together are equally justified.[6] This is obviously false too. Some proposals for hegemonic rule are better than others. Soviet communism is probably the worst. There are many other bad ones, such as a racially based fascism, and murderous theologically based regimes such as the so-called Islamic State. Once this obvious truth is accepted, it becomes possible to think of what the reasonable alternatives to liberalism are and indeed that liberalism is the best available regime that we can now conceive. Certainly, deep pluralism is not a coherent alternative. Even if we are undecided on what is the best regime, some well-ordered state is better than the chaos that would result from trying to implement the multi-culturalism of deep pluralism.

Identity-based multi-culturalism developed from a more general philosophy that flourished in the 1980s and came to be known as communitarianism. The communitarians saw themselves in their different ways as radical critics of liberalism. Their fundamental objection to what they called liberalism was its individualist character. Liberals, on this view, see society as ideally arising from, and having its content determined by, the autonomous choices of independent but equal individuals. If we can arrive at a basic structure of rules of interaction for such individuals, which they themselves as free and equal beings would rationally choose, then we would have obtained the holy grail of a just society.

The communitarians reject such a conception on the grounds that individuals are not first and foremost human beings but members of particular communities into which they are born and through which they are formed as self-identifying and reasoning beings. They come to consciousness of themselves as individuals as members of the X community before they identify themselves as members of the human race. So, although they can arrive at a universal self-consciousness, this cannot be their primary identity. Furthermore, they can learn to think about how the world is and what is good and bad in it only through the modes of thinking about these things that are present in their community. Thus, in thinking about justice, they cannot but start with what is thought about justice in their community and can seek only elaborations or transformations of these inherited ideas.

There is an obvious truth to these claims. However, whether they constitute penetrating criticisms of any liberal philosopher, I will not consider here. It suffices to point out that these errors – if they are errors – cannot apply to my account of liberalism since that account begins with individuals as members of independent political societies. Hence, their identities, interests and ideas must be presumed to have been formed through that membership. Nevertheless, there are three respects in which my approach to these issues differs from that of the communitarians. In the first place, the communitarians identify liberalism as a philosophy. This is what I call a theory of liberalism and falls in the third part of my study. Liberalism as a set of practices of the kind I discuss in the first part of this study cannot possibly be subject to the communitarian critique. For these practices exist as the rules of interaction of some actual enduring societies. So, it must be possible for a community to take a liberal form. But, then, there must be some theory of liberalism that best captures the ideas and values embedded in these practices. Liberalism, as a theory, cannot just be a series of errors.

In the second place, the communitarians have difficulty avoiding the relativist trap. It looks as though they must claim that if one is born into a liberal society, one cannot but be a liberal, and if one is born into a communist society, one cannot but be a communist, and so on. Such a view is obviously false. It ignores the fact that individuals and societies are to different degrees open to new ideas. This is possible because any particular culture, in making claims about what is true and what is valuable, necessarily opens itself to challenges on these matters from whatever source. Furthermore, in accepting that individuals can move from a communal self-identification to a universalist one, in which they can think about themselves and their societies from the perspective of being human, the communitarians must allow that the universalism present in liberal theory will be present in other forms in other cultures. Such universalist ideas cannot but assert their hegemony within the particular traditions in which they emerged.

Finally, there are two ways in which my approach involves an appeal to a universalist conception. The first is the idea of the ethical community as one in which the members commit themselves to developing rules that aim at the satisfaction of the fundamental interests of each member. This is a communitarian conception of the ethical. The idea of the ethical, according to which people commit to treating each other as ends and not merely as means, arises and only makes sense as the practice of communities. Although this is a communitarian conception of the ethical, it is at the same time a universalist idea. The second universalist element follows from the initial commitment of the members to treat each other as ends. The members' aim must be to develop rules of interaction that best realize the ethical idea.

There is another form of multi-culturalism that is liberal in character because it recognizes that groups with illiberal beliefs and values must observe the liberal constraints on what they can do and must accept that they will be at a relative disadvantage in trying to preserve their way of life in a liberal society. Yet, it still attaches great importance to cultural identity and, as an expression of egalitarian liberalism, it has quite radical implications for the relation between the national identity and the many cultural sub-groups within it. Under egalitarian liberalism each individual is of inherent and equal worth and is thereby entitled to enjoy an equality of outcome (e.g. an equality of well-being) or an equality of income or resources. These equally worthy individuals in exercising their capacity for autonomy and in accordance with their liberal rights choose to identify themselves with one or other of their society's sub-groups. Since the individual's interests are now constituted by his choice of the way of life of the X sub-group, resources will have to be poured into the X group to ensure that that individual can obtain the equality of outcome or the equality of resources to which he is entitled. In other words, the many cultures with which individuals identify themselves should be given equal treatment in order to give equal treatment to their members. This idea creates problems. Consider the issue of different language-groups. The language of the British people is English. Yet, there are many minority groups whose first language is something else. Within the British national identity there are at least two groups who think of themselves as a nation in their own right – the Welsh and the Scots. Insofar as they accept Britisn nationality, their status within that identity is as national minorities. They both have their own language. Welsh, in particular, is still a first language in some parts of Wales. Recently, Welsh has come to be given equal status with English in the public institutions in Wales and is now compulsorily taught in their schools. These developments are reasonable given that the Welsh are a historical nation with their own land and history even though their nation has long been incorporated in the multi-national independent political society that is the UK. However, the equal treatment of the Welsh language with English in Wales is not an example of the application of egalitarian liberalism since that would require the equal treatment of Welsh throughout the UK or wherever Welsh people live. It would also require the equal treatment of all the other first languages spoken by citizens of the UK.

More generally, the liberal egalitarian version of multi-culturalism would require that people of British culture should not be privileged in the institutions and policies of the British state over people belonging to minority cultures. These people are, for the most part, not long-established national minorities, like the Welsh and the

Scots with their own land and history, but fairly recent immigrants into the country. Some are refugees fleeing persecution in their own country. Most have chosen to migrate to the UK to improve their economic condition. They would seem to be under an obligation to accept the language, values and way of life of their host country insofar as that is necessary for them to obtain the advantages that they sought in migrating. Special measures to help migrants to integrate successfully into British society are obviously justified, but to suppose that the language and culture the migrants bring with them are entitled to equal treatment with British language and culture is fairly preposterous and would certainly be counter-productive. That egalitarian liberalism is so obviously untenable in this context is because it ignores the importance of national identity. This subject will be covered in the next chapter.

GROUP RIGHTS

On the view of liberalism that I have been developing in this book, the bearers of the rights that a liberal society bestows on its members are primarily individuals pursuing their individual interests by themselves or in free association with others subject to the standard constraints. Any rights that groups may acquire in this scheme have been treated as derived from the rights of their individual members. However, this claim does not and cannot apply to the individuals' membership of their independent political society. Membership of such a group is a presupposition of the individuals' possession of the liberal rights. As a result, the legitimacy of an independent political society cannot be grounded in liberal individual rights. There is indeed a historically important political theory that does attempt such a legitimation. This is the 17th- and 18th-century natural rights and social contract theory. I will discuss this theory in Part III and show why it is untenable.

There is, then, at least one group – an independent political society – that, insofar as it has rights, must possess them without deriving them from the prior rights of its members. Such a group must have rights of some kind since by its very constitution it claims the authority to establish and enforce binding rules of interaction on its members. Where does it get that authority from? Very briefly, we should understand this authority as emerging as a practice in which a collection of people come to acknowledge the right of a person or a body of persons to establish such binding rules. However, the practice requires that the ruling authority in its legislative and executive activity seeks to protect and promote the fundamental interests of each member as well as the interests of the group as a whole. So understood, the practice that has emerged is that of an ethical community that possesses inherent authority over its members. The authority rests on agreement among the members in the manner of practices in general, not as a formal contract but as a way of living together that develops its forms and principles over time. It may be said also to be grounded in the fundamental interests of the members although not in their rights.

This independent political society with inherent authority over its members has in itself no rights against other independent political societies. Any such rights must emerge as part of another practice in which a society of such groups comes to recognize its members' sovereignty along the lines that already exist in international law and which I discuss in the next chapter.

Since the liberal idea does not exclude, and in fact must presuppose, the existence of at least one group right, could there exist other groups within liberal society whose authority over their members is not entirely dependent on their members' prior individual rights? I believe so. In the first place, the family is such a group. The existence of families in some form would seem to be essential to the survival and well-functioning of an independent political society over time. I understand a family as a very small group of adults possessing special rights and duties in regard to the upbringing of their children. These children may have been adopted, produced with the help of an independent donor or by heterosexual acts. The importance of the family grouping arises, not only from its being probably the best way to care for the physical and emotional needs of the political society's children but also because it is the way in which the children are first introduced to an understanding of what it is to be a member of an ethical grouping in which claims against other members are balanced by duties to them. A family is, in other words, an ethical community in its own right on a small scale but one in which up to a certain age one section has a dependent status on the other. As an ethical grouping the collectivity has inherent rights over its members derived from its nature and function as a family and not from the prior rights of its members.

The prosperity of its families is a fundamental interest of the independent political society, and hence it should protect and promote them. But it has this interest and duty not as a liberal society but as a society tout court. In a liberal society enjoying sexual freedom, families standardly come into existence through the exercise by individuals of their freedom rights. But what they bring into existence has an underlying nature and function which binds their wills.

Are there other groups in society that have a similar ethical status to families? Not exactly, since families contain the form of ethical communities in miniature. But insofar as one can identify a specific function that a type of grouping fulfils in the larger society, the grouping may be held to have an authority over its members that is not derived simply from the will of individuals to associate on terms of their choosing. Thus universities should be understood as organizations for the development and transmission of knowledge about the physical and social worlds. The existence and well-functioning of such organizations are of fundamental importance to independent political societies in the modern age. The operation of these societies is now massively dependent on producing sufficient members with the scientific and social knowledge to manage them and compete successfully with other such societies. Thus, the state has an interest and duty to promote them. But, once again this is an interest it has simply as a state and not as a liberal state. In a liberal society, individuals must be free to join such organizations if they possess the relevant qualifications and leave them if they wish. But, once they have joined as students or faculty, they are necessarily subject to the authority contained in them that is derived from their nature as developers and transmitters of knowledge. How they are to be financed is an open question. But it is absurd to treat them as though they were just supermarkets of knowledge offering intellectual goods to individual consumers. Furthermore, the best way to promote the acquisition of knowledge is by developing a love for it independently of its utility as one motivation among others.

Museums and other arts organizations, religious groups, trade unions and employers' federations may or may not be understood as serving special functions in society and be candidates for similar treatment to universities. Insofar as a case can be made out for these groups' special function in serving a fundamental interest of the society in its survival and well-functioning, the society may have a duty to promote their establishment and prospering. Some people believe that cultural groups that exist to defend and promote their distinctive cultures have a special function and should be supported by the state. So, the state should foster Hindu culture, Muslim culture, Afghan culture and so on. This is a mistake. The state has an interest in promoting the cultivation of the arts, but its concern here is not with any distinctive ethnicity's traditions but with excellence in the arts. Similarly, its concern in promoting science is not with Hindu science or Muslim science or British science but with science in Britain by whomsoever can best achieve excellence in it. Thus also with sport.

Culture as used by these promoters of state-supported multiculturalism, of course, does not mean the cultivation of the arts but the values and way of life of a distinct ethnicity. However, the state has no business promoting the values and way of life of any people except those of its own. This means that a liberal state has no business promoting other than its liberal values and way of life. In the sense to be discussed in the next chapter, its overriding object of concern on issues of identity is with its own national identity — the identity of its own people. Nevertheless, it is also true that if there are large numbers of people of diverse origins and ethnicities in a society, the national identity must accommodate them in some way.

FURTHER READING

On equality in general, a good introduction is White (2007). See also the essays in Mason (1998) and for contemporary egalitarianism, see Kymlicka (1990).

For a critique of modern ideas of equality, see Charvet (2013) and Lloyd Thomas (1979).

On equality of status, see Miller (1998), Anderson (1999) and Wolff (1998).

On sufficientism, see Frankfurt (1987).

On liberal feminism, see Charvet (1982), Friedan (1965).

For difference feminism, see Gilligan (1983), Weedon (1999) and I.M. Young (1990).

Post-modern feminism, read Butler (1990).

For identity multi-culturalism, see Connolly (2005) and Appiah (2005).

The main communitarian thinkers are Sandel (1982), MacIntyre (1981), Taylor (1985) (1990) and Walzer (1983, 1987, 1994).

On communitarianism, read Mulhall and Swift (1996). On group rights, read Jones (2016).

NOTES

1 Rousseau (1968, p.99). What he actually said was "each citizen shall be at the same time perfectly independent of all his fellow citizens and excessively dependent on the republic". His extreme formulation is typical and unwarranted.
2 Locke (1964) 2nd Treatise, para 54.
3 Temkin (1993, pp.247–8).
4 Aristotle (1921) 1254B.
5 Lacey (2004, p.27).
6 Strictly speaking, they would all be equally UNjustified. On that basis, one might just as well opt for the existing dominant culture.

COMMUNITY

INDEPENDENT POLITICAL SOCIETY

By community I mean, in this context, the common identity, sentiments and interests that members of the same independent political society must have to a certain degree if that society is to survive and flourish. First of all, by independent political society I mean a territorial entity that is under the control of a government in the sense that the government can make and enforce decisions regarding the rules and policies that inhabitants of that territory are to follow. While that government may be more or less strongly influenced in its decision-making by outside powers, it is nevertheless independent if it claims, accepts and is acknowledged to have, responsibility for the rules and policies that are to apply to the people in its territory. In other words, it has the form of a sovereign state. Older political forms, such as ancient kingdoms and empires, may have had looser connections between the central ruler and outlying parts of their territories than the idea of the sovereign state implies. But at least for core regions of the territory, the ruler must be in a position to decide and enforce the rules and policies governing his people's interactions if he is to be said to be the authoritative ruler of that area.

In the second place, for this independent entity to count as a political society, the ruler must claim that the people are morally obliged to obey the rules and policies that he issues because he is authorized in some way (by God, heredity, tradition, nature, the nation or the people) to take decisions for their good. A band of heavily armed thugs could take over a territory and establish by force procedures for exploiting its inhabitants. Such rulers would not claim any community between them and their subjects. They would make no pretence of acting for their subjects' good or acknowledge among themselves any bond other than their common interest in exploiting the producers of wealth. Since it is easy to make ethical claims without doing anything to substantiate them if you are powerful enough, it is unlikely that my thugs would not engage in the process of rationalizing their oppression. So, it may well be difficult to identify the genuine article. Such hypocrisy, however, is, as La Rochefoucauld said, the tribute that vice pays to virtue.[1] Also, words have consequences: some people may believe them and start acting as though they were true.

Assuming, then, that we are talking about the genuine thing, a political society necessarily aspires to a conception of a common good that unites ruler and people. The ruler's authority, and so his good, rests in part on his having as his aim the good of his subjects in issuing particular rules and policies. This common good, furthermore, supposes that the ruler and people possess a common identity. They share a common political space. It is their political society. The people may be united only as subjects of the monarch. Their unity is constituted through this common subjection. For them, we, the people means we, the subjects of the Tsar or whatever his title is. But the monarch is only monarch as ruler of these people. The monarch is "our" monarch and the people are "his" people.

In the modern state God and Monarch have largely retreated as authority creators and bearers, and it is the people through some actual or fictitious election of their representatives who bestow authority on the legislators and policy-makers. The people, consequently, have become ultimate rulers as well as subjects and hence fully occupy without division the political space that is their political society. Their common identity consists formally in the fact that they together constitute the ruling entity as well as the subjects unified by this rule. We, the people, is now primarily an assertion of their authority to rule a certain territory and secondarily an affirmation of their unity as the intended beneficiaries of this rule. It is rule of the people by the people for the people.[2] This formal common identity is, however, of no use unless there exists a substantive common identity that is sufficiently pervasive in the population of the territory that is formally united under one rule to give effect to the idea of a sovereign people in this area. Their formal unity may be belied by irreconcilable differences of an ethnic, religious, national or political nature.

In the next section I will discuss the main options for understanding the possibility of achieving in the modern world a sufficiently substantive common identity for the effective rule of a people claiming sovereign authority in a territory. But first I must reiterate why I think it is necessary, in an introductory book on what liberalism is, to engage with problems of political community. I have emphasized all along that liberalism at the most basic level consists in a set of practices adopted as authoritative rules of interaction for its members by an independent political society or state or recommended for adoption by such an independent political society. Thus, the liberal practices presuppose the existence of such a society. Hence, we must interpret the liberal principles in that context. From that point of view, it would be absurd to elaborate an account of liberal practices as though they could exist in a world without states. We need to know the conditions of existence of such societies, especially in the modern world in which liberalism has emerged as a political option, in order to understand the limits on a viable interpretation of the liberal idea of an equal freedom. Such limitations were indeed assumed in Part I under the rubric of national security, and this chapter is a justification and elaboration of the idea that there is such a thing as a nation politically organized in a state whose interests need defending.

However, a qualification has to be made to this line of argument. There are some libertarians, and thus on my understanding liberals, who are anarchists. They believe that the libertarian view of an equal freedom can be realized best in a world without states. They see liberal practices as rules of interaction for independent individuals in what used to be called a state of nature and would be a pre- or post-political state. I shall consider this claim briefly in Part III when evaluating libertarian theory. For now, I will proceed in the next sections to discuss the problems of a world of states on the assumption that people need to associate in societies under common rules backed by a force that claims authority to act on behalf of the society as a whole.

LIBERALISM AND NATIONAL IDENTITY

The presupposition of this chapter – indeed a presupposition of the whole book – is that a political society requires an authority that claims the right and responsibility for enunciating and enforcing common rules for the members. In the modern world this authority is grounded in the people who constitute its members. This is true, of course, of liberal-democracies but also of communist states, which identify the people with the workers, and fascist or semi-fascist states, which identify the people with the nation. In the anti-democracies there is some pretence made, through managed elections or referenda, for the people to bestow their authority on the actual leaders. In the liberal-democracies the genuineness of the elections depends on the creation and maintenance of the conditions necessary for the elections to be fair, open and free. There are, indeed, some religious autocracies, such as Iran and Saudi Arabia. These are relics of another world and are theocracies in which God is supposed to rule through his specially designated agents.

The problem of political authority in the modern world, in which the ultimate sovereign is supposed to be the people, is how to distribute the population of the world between states in a way that provides the members of each state with a sufficiently robust substantive common identity to sustain their formal unity as the sovereign will in their state. This, of course, presumes that we need a plurality of states. It is possible that at some time in the future there will come into existence an effective world state. But at the moment it is difficult to conceive of this other than as an oppressive world empire of one state such as China or the United States, and difficult to think of such a world empire coming about before the destruction of the world in a nuclear war. At present, we have a world of states which seek to cooperate, through the United Nations and other international organizations, with varying degrees of sincerity, effort and success in creating and maintaining peaceful and profitable interaction. I shall assume this context for the rest of this chapter.[3]

A major reason why we need a plurality of states is because the peoples of the world are so diverse in their beliefs, values and cultures that it is very difficult to conceive of them being unified in a single political system even if that system had a federal structure with considerable autonomy for its parts. Some long-established nation-states such as the UK and Spain are currently having problems in maintaining the cohesion of their regions. The European Union, composed at present of 27 states (after the exit of the UK in March 2019) all supposedly committed to the beliefs and values of liberal-democracy, staggers along held together by a powerful but unpopular bureaucracy. Hence, it seems reasonable to say that an effective world state is not conceivable under present conditions except as an oppressive empire of the most powerful state or combination of states over the others.

So, we need a plurality of states in order to organize politically the diversity of peoples. It follows that we cannot simply divide up the world into different territorial entities without regard to the coherence of the peoples corralled together by these boundaries and expect them to share their allocated political space in an effective and reasonably harmonious way. Such a world is more or less what the retreating European empires left behind them in Africa when they abandoned the territories they had carved out for themselves in their own interests to the arbitrary collection of peoples they had unified as their subjects. The results have been dire. This suggests strongly that in considering how the world should be divided into separate states, we should pay attention to the important commonalities that already exist or that can reasonably be created. The presence of such actual or possible commonalities is standardly conceptualized as a nation. On this view, given that we need a plurality of states, their boundaries should be drawn as much as possible to correspond with the existence or promotion of national identities.

The trouble is that what a nation is, is not a very determinate concept. Some people believe that there are clearly delineated collectivities called nations, that each nation should have its own state, and that the world would be a better and more peaceful one once this has come about. Yet, even if one is not a fully fledged nationalist in these terms, one may well believe that the idea of a nation is an important notion for promoting the sort of coherence and unity among a collection of people that is necessary for creating and maintaining a viable political society in the modern world.

What do the nationalists think constitutes a nation? Standardly, they distinguish objective factors from subjective ones. Objective factors are ethno-cultural commonalities such as a common ancestry, language, religion, culture, history and common occupation of a territory. The subjective factor is the belief by persons who possess some or all of these commonalities that in virtue of this common possession they constitute a nation with special obligations to one another arising from the value inherent in a nation and with legitimate aspirations to be politically self-governing. One problem with the nationalist's account is that the commonalities may be present without the subjective factor of belief that the presence of the objective factors gave them special obligations to each other and entitled them to be self-governing. There were nations in the objective sense long before nationalism in the subjective sense arose. Nationalism in the subjective sense is an invention of the 18th and 19th centuries. Another problem is that there are successful political collectivities whose members think of themselves as a nation but who possess few, if any, of the commonalities identified as making a nation e.g. the Americans, the British, the Swiss, the Spanish. Indeed, most nation-states have been in the business of forging among their citizens a sense of unity out of a variegated ethnic and cultural material. The new states of Eastern Europe and Africa that arose from the dismantlement of the European and Ottoman empires in the course of the 19th and 20th centuries have had and still have Herculean tasks in this respect.

Because the objective commonalities uniting a people may be very limited, and the subjective factor of belief by the members that this collection of people constituting together a political community with special obligations to each other may be much more important, it is tempting to do away with the objective factors altogether and to define a nation just in terms of a collection of individuals unified through a political constitution. The constitution of an independent state bestows a common identity on the members of the collection and gives them special rights and duties which they do not have in relation to non-members. This temptation should be resisted. It is extremely unlikely that mere constitutional unity would be sufficient in normal conditions to create the solidarity that is supposed to be provided by the objective commonalities that contribute to the making of a nation. Very threatening external circumstances may drive such a collection to pull together and over time to sustain an independent political society. But it is probable that establishing such an entity in the first place would require a nucleus of objective commonalities to which more disparate ethnic and cultural material could attach itself just as the nucleus of the American people was provided by the settlers of British descent who led the revolt against their British government. British national identity is itself a concoction of largely English and Celtic peoples together with admixtures of Vikings and Normans to which further large numbers of immigrants from around the world have recently attached their own identities. It is further complicated by the fact that the Scots – themselves composed of Irish, Picts, English and Vikings – had formed their own national identity before they united themselves with the English to create the United Kingdom of Great Britain and the British national identity. Likewise, the Welsh think of themselves as a nation and have their own language and history as an independent entity.

All these considerations strongly suggest that the notion of a nation and national identity is very flexible. It covers collectivities that may not have any political standing or aspiration to such standing. Thus, as noted earlier, collectivities such as the English, the Germans, the Irish existed and were referred to as nations long before the term came to be associated with political ambitions of self-government. But the term now has a significant political connotation: a nation is presumed to have a claim to a degree of self-government. What brought about this addition was the change in the course of the 18th and 19th centuries in the understanding of the location of the source of political authority: not the Monarch but the people. This immediately created the problem of which collection of individuals is to count as the people entitled to constitute themselves as the source of political authority in a territory? There were only two answers to that question: the population already collected as subjects of the Monarch or some other collection with a sense of their common identity. That other could only be the nation already existing such as the Irish, the Germans and so on. The trouble was that many of the existing territorial units had minority populations. Ireland had significant numbers of people of Scottish and English descent. So either the territory had to be partitioned or the understanding of the national identity had to be modified to include the minority populations in it. This is the point at which the notion of the nation can become restrictive and divisive or flexible and expansive. It will tend to the former if the content of national identity is focused on ethnicity with the result, for example, that because Jews did not count as Germans for the Nazi regime, even if they had German citizenship and were imbued with German culture, it was believed that they had to be excised from the German nation. If the focus is on the unifying elements of culture, then, since this notion is fairly flexible itself, it can accommodate diverse ethnicities and a changing content.

The appeal to a national identity of some kind, then, is an unavoidable accompaniment of the commitment to popular sovereignty in modern states. National identity must be forged, maintained or allowed to evolve but must be given some content. This content may be thoroughly illiberal. If the emphasis is on ethnicity, the content will tend to be illiberal. If the emphasis is on culture, then its liberality will depend on the culture. A liberal culture will be characterized by its respect for the liberal freedoms. Because of this respect, the culture and so the national identity will be much more flexible and subject to change than would an illiberal national culture. But it cannot be so flexible that the people lose a sense of who they are. One obvious way in which this can be done is through massive and rapid immigration. Another way in which a people can lose their sense of identity is through substantial loss of power and prestige in the international order. They will be subject to dreams of taking back control or of making their country great again when what is really required is an adjustment of their sense of their place in the new balance of power. In general, the leaders of a polity must pay attention in the policies they pursue to the need for the cohesion of the "we" that grounds their authority.

LIBERALISM AND INTERNATIONAL SOCIETY

We are assuming, then, that we are living in an independent political society that has chosen to organize itself internally on the basis of liberal-democratic social and political norms and is one such society among many others occupying an international realm. The members of our state are under obligation to each other to interact on the basis of the liberal norms and values. But what are their obligations to the members of other states? The answer to that depends on the nature of the international realm. It must have an ethical character if the members of one state are to be ethically obliged to the members of other states.

Some of these other states will be liberal-democracies like your own, but others will not be. They may be rabidly hostile with the intention to undermine and destroy your independence or maybe only your liberal-democratic order, which may be perceived by the leaders of the hostile states as a threat to their own existence as leaders of illiberal and autocratic regimes. Other illiberal or only partially liberal states may be merely suspicious of the liberal states' agenda and may seek to contain their ideologically aggrandizing efforts. In these circumstances your state must have a foreign policy. It must decide how to conduct its relations with other liberal states and with the variety of illiberal states. Since there are heavily armed hostile states in the international environment, part of your state's foreign policy will have to take the form of building up its armed forces on its own and through military alliances with friendly states.

Given the recurrent level of hostility between states and the not infrequent recourse to war to settle disputes, some thinkers treat the international realm as a morally free zone in which each state is entitled to do whatever it believes is best from the point of view of its own long-term interest. Thus, if it thinks its security in the long run will be best secured by smashing its rivals in open warfare, then this is what it should and will do. But it may believe that the balance of power is such that it would do better for itself by trying to maintain international peace through preserving the balance. That way the potentially warring states are mutually deterred from engaging in such risky adventures. However, should the balance tip in your favour, your previous commitments to preserve the balance are irrelevant and may be morally and strategically ignored.

These thinkers are called realists, and they repudiate the idea that the international realm is any kind of society governed by ethical norms. If the international realm is correctly identified as a morally free zone, then indeed no state will have any moral obligations to the other states. But would the same apply to the members of one of these states to the members of other states? Surely, they should be committed at the least to respecting each other's basic rights to life, liberty, property and contract? But if you undertake to trade in a foreign territory and the state owner of the territory is entitled to seize your goods should it believe it to be in its interests and allows its members to rob or kill you with impunity, your rights in your property and your life in the foreign state are not worth very much, and in those circumstances your obligations would not be worth very much either. So, if there is going to be an international civil society in which individuals and associations of individuals from the different states are able to interact commercially and culturally with a sufficient degree of security to make such interactions worthwhile, the states must treat the foreigners entering their territory as entitled to the protection of their laws. But if the states are in the business of promoting the legal protection of their citizens in each other's territories, they must be committed to creating an international realm in which the states respect each other's territory and legal order so that their citizens can move with some degree of freedom in the space provided by such mutual respect.

Many people believe that such a world with those aspirations actually exists. It is called an international society or society of states and has laws and courts staffed with highly paid lawyers to regulate it. It is recognized to have serious problems, and substantial efforts have been made to overcome these problems. The realists deny that anyone is obliged by these so-called laws since there is no international police force to enforce them but only the forces of self-interested other states. For the realists, international law is a form through which some states seek to pursue their own interests. But it always has escape clauses that enable non-conforming states to deny that they are in violation of its rules. Since the enforcement of its provisions depends on the other states, you only have to be powerful enough to deter them in order to get away with your supposedly illegal actions. Thus, international law now makes the waging of aggressive war illegal. The leaders of Nazi Germany were prosecuted and condemned at the Nuremberg trials after WWII for this crime. But an aggressor state only has to claim that it was acting in self-defence to impose on the other states the burden of waging war to enforce the rule. If Germany had won the war, the Nazi leaders would obviously have escaped prosecution and condemnation and would have executed the leaders of the liberal-democracies.

The anti-realists are called liberals. But liberalism in this context does not mean that you are in favour of the liberal freedoms for the domestic organization of your state. It means that you believe that the international realm is constituted to a certain degree as a genuine society governed by norms. It is, of course, an anarchical society in which there is no sovereign body to determine authoritatively what the law is and powerful enough to enforce it. Instead, the laws are understood to be revealed in the customary practices of states which the states themselves accept as binding on them, in multi-lateral treaties such as the treaty produced by The Congress of Vienna, the League of Nations and especially the United Nations Treaty[4] and in a succession of bilateral treaties, agreements, official statements and diplomatic acts. The fundamental norms of this international society recognize the independence, autonomy and territorial integrity of each state — in other words its sovereignty. To recognize the sovereignty of a state in regard to a territory is to accept that the state is in a position to create and maintain a legal and political order in that territory, that it is entitled to establish any internal order it wishes and that other states are to respect its right. If the facts of sovereign control of each territory are accurate and its rights are respected, there would exist an international society consisting of diverse legal and political jurisdictions with some commonalities in regard to the rules which would enable appropriately informed commercial and other travellers to navigate their way around without fear of destitution or persecution.

Another fundamental principle of this international society is said to be the principle of pacta sunt servanda (treaties are to be kept). Clearly, there would not be much point in drawing up elaborate bilateral and multi-lateral agreements if it was not implicit in them that their provisions had to be kept. This principle would seem to contradict the realist contention that international law does not oblige. However, the realist believes that it is always possible to evade the obligation by claiming that the circumstances have changed sufficiently for the treaty no longer to apply and by daring the other parties to go to war to maintain their right. It is now possible to take disputes to the International Court at The Hague. But a classic example of the realist case is the recent dismissal by the Court of the Chinese claim to several offshore uninhabited islands and reefs in the South China Sea that are far closer to the territories of Vietnam and the Philippines than they are to China. China has simply rejected the Court's judgement as politically motivated and continues to construct military posts on them. Even the United States is not in a position to stop them.

Probably the best view of the international realm is that it is a mixture of norm-governed societal and realist elements. There are international laws and institutions and an international civil society that operates in an orderly and peaceful manner a good deal of the time. But because it is at best an anarchical society in which the states are the enforcers of the norms, each state ultimately has to rely on its own forces and those of what allies it can secure in order to ensure that its interests are preserved. In this respect it approaches the conception of the international system embraced by the realists.

A liberal state, then, has to seek to protect and promote its interests in such a context. The United Nations Treaty has complicated this context to some degree. The treaty re-emphasizes the sovereignty norms of international law but has introduced new constraints on the exercise of that sovereignty although without providing any effective mechanism for ensuring that they are observed. These constraints are spelled out in its Universal Declaration of Human Rights of 1948 and in the subsequent international covenants on political and civil rights and social and economic rights that elaborated the principles affirmed in the universal declaration and have been signed and ratified by most states. The promotion of respect for these rights has now become the official policy of the United Nations Organization and hence part of international law. While some of the rights could be endorsed by any reasonable rule of law-abiding but illiberal state, many of the civil and political rights could be accepted only by states committed to liberal-democratic institutions. On this basis it looked as though international society as reconstructed after WWII had transformed itself into a society of actual and aspiring liberal states. But given that a good number of members were in fact dictatorships of various kinds – communist, religious, military, or merely authoritarian – this was bound to be illusory. One must suppose that these states signed and ratified the human rights treaties only because they were confident that they could subvert or ignore them. They were right. For many years the UN did little to promote human rights other than issue declarations and covenants. Subsequently, when the newly independent former colonies began to arrive on the international scene, the UN set up special committees to investigate and remedy human rights abuses. But the main object of concern of these committees turned out not to be the dictatorships or indeed the newly independent states, which for the most part abandoned quickly enough their liberal inheritance from the colonial powers, but the remaining colonial or supposedly colonial situations of which the Israeli occupied territories in Palestine and the apartheid regime in South Africa were the main targets. While colonial and racist regimes are of obvious concern to liberals, the overall effect of the UN Human Rights regime has been deeply disappointing for them.

The UN treaty also introduced a potentially powerful governing body for international society – its Security Council. This body can make decisions that are binding on all the members. It is composed of five permanent members, each of whom can veto a resolution passed by the remaining members of the council, and ten non-permanent members who are elected for a two-year term. The permanent members are China, France, Russia, the UK and the United States. They are supposed to be the great powers. The UN Charter thus allows for the rule of the great powers over the rest provided they can agree among themselves and secure three non-permanent members to support them. In fact, the great powers have very rarely been in agreement. While the Security Council has authorized some useful peace-making and peace-keeping initiatives in places where the great powers have not been in confrontation, it has made little difference to the fundamental situation of an independent sovereign state in a world of such states. You still have to look to your own security with what allies you can find.

In these circumstances, how should a liberal state conduct its foreign policy, first of all towards fellow liberal states and second, towards illiberal states, some of which may be powerful and hostile? There are two main strategies possible here: one is to create a society of liberal states that would operate independently of the wider international society, which would be constructed much as it is at present; the other is to commit to a single international society composed of liberal and illiberal states that would recognize some minimal version of rights acceptable to the illiberal states.

A separately organized society of liberal states would first of all be a military alliance in which the members undertook to come to each other's aid should they be attacked. In the second place, it would seek to protect and promote liberal values both internally within the society and externally by attracting new members. However, it should be absolutely clear that it is in intention a military alliance for defence only and not expansion. The attraction of new members would be achieved through the manifestation to outsiders of the advantages of the liberal way of life in terms of the peace, prosperity and civility that it brings. The great advantage of such a society of liberal states would be the creation of an international civil society based on liberal commonalities. The members of each state would be able to move freely around this society enjoying the liberal freedoms without fear of being used as a pawn in some power game between states and losing their property, liberty or life. The promotion of liberalism internally would include setting minimum common standards for all members to reach and through the judgements of a court regarding compliance with such standards by member states. The wealthier liberal states would be expected to help the weaker liberal states attain these standards. Such a society would be something of a cross between NATO and the EU. But it would be a confederation of independent states and in no sense a federal state in its own right. It would be embedded in the larger international society whose features would be much the same as exist now. It would, of course, constitute a powerful bloc of states which is likely to be seen as threatening by the illiberal states, much as the leaders of Russia view NATO and the west today.

The alternative for the liberal states is to continue as at present. Within the single international society there would be military alliances like NATO and the hybrid state that is the EU. There would be the UN with its official commitment to a liberal-democratic human rights programme but its actual hopeless weakness in protecting and advancing such values. International civil society will be composed of different types of legal orders within the territories of each state. Members of liberal states travelling in the spaces governed by illiberal legal orders may find that they have no rights to practise their religion, to associate with whom they please or to speak freely, and the security of their life, liberty and property under a rule of law may be very uncertain. Members of illiberal states travelling within the liberal territories, however, will enjoy all these advantages.

International society under either of these scenarios would remain a highly dangerous place, with many states, not well-disposed to each other, armed to the teeth with enormously destructive weapons.

FURTHER READING

On sovereignty, read Krasner (1999). On nationalism, read Smith (2001), Moore (2001) and particularly Miller (2007).

Bull (1977) is a classic account of international society. See also Watson (1972).

On realism in international relations, see Donnelly (2000).

Held (1995) is an attempt to envisage a global democracy.

On international law, read any standard textbook such as Dixon (2000).

On all the issues in this chapter, see Charvet and Kaczynska-Nay (2008).

NOTES

1 La Rochefoucauld was a 17th-century French writer famous for his aphorisms. See La Rochefoucauld, Maxims (1981).
2 President Lincoln's famous words after the civil war battle of Gettysburg in 1863 that saved the northern cause.
3 However, Donald Trump, elected president of the United States in 2017, the leader of the most powerful state in the world, looks as though he believes that multi-lateral cooperation between states of any kind is bad for the United States and that he can obtain better deals through bilateral treaties. Such a policy would not be very clever. It would only harm the United States and its allies and benefit China.
4 The Congress of Vienna (1814–15), consisting of the representatives of the European states, agreed a new order for Europe after the disruptions of the French revolutionary and Napoleonic wars. The League of Nations was established at the end of WWI with the aim of ensuring the peaceful settlement of international disputes. It was a dismal failure and was replaced at the end of WWII by the United Nations Organization.

LIBERALISM AND HUMAN WELL-BEING

THE MEANING OF WELL-BEING

If the reorganization of one's society along liberal lines could be shown probably to lead to the immiseration of its members, then there would be little reason to embrace it. So, the question must be raised as to whether the introduction of liberalism has or is likely to have such consequences. Well-being is not, of course, a specifically liberal value and is included in this Part of the book on liberal values because it is a fundamental human value with which all other values must be connected and hence liberal values also. Individuals seek their well-being and associate in various types of society with a view to promoting their well-being. However, the notion of well-being can be distinguished into various elements such as material, spiritual, moral, associational and no doubt many other possible sub-divisions. So, this chapter is likely to be found unsatisfactory from many different points of view. Nevertheless, I must attempt to give a sketch of how liberalism can be reasonably defended in terms of a plausible conception of human well-being.

First of all some general considerations about the notion of well-being. I shall assume that another way of talking about the well-being of an entity is in terms of its flourishing. Thus, to determine whether an entity such as a tree is doing well or not, we have to have an idea of what the conditions for trees in general to do well are and whether there are any special conditions for this particular type of tree. And so on for the various types of living being. So, to begin with, we have to take a view of what sort of being a human being is. Some parts of the answer are easy enough – a human being is a social animal. To flourish he needs food, shelter, reproductive conditions and membership of a pack. But he is also a rational animal. By this I mean that he has developed, through his association with others in language-speaking communities, the ability to subject his unreflective beliefs and actions to the power of reasons – reasons for believing and reasons for acting. Since the possession of this power defines what it is to be a human social animal, among the conditions of human flourishing must be included a good state of his reasoning powers.

LIBERALISM AND MATERIAL WELL-BEING

Human beings have used these powers among other things to improve vastly their material conditions of life beyond their original animal state. So, what it takes for a human being to flourish materially under present day conditions probably includes ease of access to motor transport, air travel, television, the Internet, innumerable domestic appliances and refined foods. Access to these things can be enjoyed at different levels, and the natural inequalities to be found in pack life have been magnified into huge inequalities of condition in human societies. At this point judgements start becoming difficult. The inequalities of society affect the level of well-being enjoyed by different members independently of the material conditions actually enjoyed. One doesn't have to accept fully Rousseau's claim that the rich are only happy so long as the poor remain poor to see that inequality per se is likely to make some happy and others unhappy.[1] This effect applies across all societies both liberal and illiberal, ancient and modern. But some people believe its effect will be worse in societies that are not formally stratified by birth into distinct social orders. In meritocracies in which everyone enjoys a formal equality of status and your position in the social order is due to your merit or lack of merit, you have nobody to blame but yourself if you find yourself at the bottom. This belief seems unlikely to be true given the level of contempt for the lower orders felt by the members of the superior classes to be found in stratified societies. In any case, since all modern societies are committed, in principle, to the unstratified model of social organization, whether they are liberal or illiberal, because they are all grounded in some version of the sovereignty of the people and because of their need to utilize the talents of their members in improving their economic performance in an intensely competitive world, the claim will have to be ignored.

If a source of feeling well and feeling ill is to be found in the existence of inequality of condition in society, do some societies do better than others in this respect by having a lower degree of inequality? In particular, do liberal societies do better than illiberal societies? There is some evidence that liberal Scandinavian societies, which enjoy a greater degree of equality than other liberal societies, score higher on well-being measures. But this evidence is hardly relevant to the choice between liberalism and illiberalism when the most unequal societies on earth are not liberal but illiberal ones.

However, the problem of material inequality is not simply about some people having more income and wealth than others. It is the reflection of that inequality in the respect a person has for herself and others have for her. It is about relative status. Some people think that all such inequalities are malign in any activity. It is wrong that some should be winners and others losers in sport, art, knowledge, commerce, politics, beauty and so on. All should get the same prize. Such small-minded stupidity gives equality a bad name and leads to the assertion of its opposite – the inherent goodness of superiority and inferiority. Excellence in any (legal) activity should be celebrated but in such a way that those who do not do so well can maintain their self-respect to a sufficient degree that their well-being is not seriously affected. Their contributions have to be valued too rather than denigrated and despised. This is the ideal of the stratified society. Everyone has a function and in fulfilling it achieves her good. Since an open, competitive, liberal society tends to the other extreme of making everybody run the same race for a better or worse position in it, how is respect for all to be maintained? First of all by valuing the different functions performed in society, however they come to be filled. Second, by attaching special weight to the equality of status everyone is supposed to enjoy as a citizen with the same basic legal and political rights as everyone else. Third, by ensuring that everyone's material condition is sufficiently good that she enjoys enough valuable options to be able to think of herself correctly as running her own life.

These considerations, together with the evidence regarding the greater level of well-being that the members of the more equal Scandinavian societies enjoy, strongly support the sufficientist view of liberal equality. It is certainly to be preferred to the libertarian on the grounds of general well-being. Also, since the egalitarian conception is so implausible, it should be the one to be adopted with a generous rather than mean-spirited interpretation of the sufficiency criterion. In any case, as liberal societies are, in general, the ones with the highest material conditions of life at the moment and are at the very least no more unequal than illiberal societies, liberalism can hardly be rejected on the grounds of its tendency to produce the material immiseration, or the material-related immiseration, of its members.

RATIONAL POWERS, AUTONOMY AND WELL-BEING

I claimed earlier that the well-being of an entity has to be considered in terms of the conditions for such a being to flourish. Since human beings are to be understood as rational, social animals, they need appropriate conditions for the successful exercise of their rational powers as well as for the satisfaction of their social and material needs. By rational powers I mean the ability to give and demand reasons for believing claims about how the world is and how one should act in it. By the power of such reasoning, human beings are able to exercise some degree of control over their unreflective beliefs and actions. In exercising such control, they develop their autonomy. Thus, a condition for human beings to flourish is that their autonomous powers are enabled to develop to their full extent and yet remain in harmony with their material and social conditions. I have already discussed what human beings' autonomous powers are in respect of reasoning about actions. Autonomy in respect of action can be developed at two levels: the first level consists in being able to successfully, but uncritically, apply a scheme of values that one has formed to the running of one's own life. The second level of autonomy consists in turning the reflective powers on those values and subjecting them to a critical evaluation. One may come to endorse them as the best way for human beings to live or modify or reject them for some other scheme.

Given that both levels are possible, what sort of society will be best for human beings depends on how one thinks these powers are distributed among individuals. If one believes that some people cannot even achieve the first level of autonomy, as used to be the view of women in the hierarchical societies of the past, then a patriarchal organization of women's place in the family and society would be appropriate.[2] If one believes, further, that second level autonomy is achievable only by an intellectual elite, one will adopt a Platonic view of how society should be organized in which philosophers should rule. If not philosophers, at least an elite that possesses special knowledge, perhaps obtained from God, as to the values around which society should be organized.

Obviously, adherents of liberalism have got to believe that everyone is capable of achieving first level autonomy. Actually, since it is clear that these powers come in degrees, we do not have to believe that all possess the powers to the same degree. What has to be true is that the vast majority possess them to a sufficient degree that their lives will go better for them – they will achieve a higher level of well-being – if they possess the liberal freedoms to run their own lives than if they are treated as natural dependents subject to the authoritative control of another for their own good. There are no doubt always some people who want to have their options limited by others and to be dominated and led by them. However, the issue is whether they would be better off by not having this want satisfied but by having confidence in their natural rational powers to take charge of their own lives under suitable material conditions. My bottom point here is that if you have this ability you will be better off exercising it, other things being equal, than having it stifled, because this is the essential human power.

What do liberals have to believe about the distribution of second level autonomy? On the assumption that the vast majority of citizens are capable of attaining a sufficient degree of first level autonomy to operate successfully in a liberal society, and have had liberal beliefs and values instilled in them through their education, it might seem possible to run a liberal society effectively with only an elite body of liberal philosophers capable of exercising second level autonomy. The elite would control the belief system of the society and discourage the ordinary citizen from thinking critically about it. The latter's role would be to run their own private lives in enjoying the liberal freedoms and leave the business of the collectivity to the elite.

Almost certainly such an arrangement would not work. In the first place, it would not be a democracy, so the democratic controls on the abuse of power by the members of the elite would be absent. Power without accountability will corrupt its possessors. But more importantly, the exercise of the major liberal freedoms of free speech, association and movement cannot but result in the development and expression among the ordinary people of beliefs and values of all kinds, including anti-liberal ones. The liberal elite could not prevent this flourishing of second level thinking among the people without violating the liberal freedoms themselves and so undermining their own claim to rule. Furthermore, if the people have been discouraged in their education from any critical thinking about liberalism, they will be vulnerable to the attacks on liberalism that are bound to arise through the exercise of the liberal freedoms. So, if liberal society is to be reasonably stable and the ordinary citizens are to be capable of resisting intellectually the siren voices of anti-liberal propaganda, they must be supposed to possess in sufficient degree a capacity for second level autonomy and to have had that capacity developed through their education.

The danger to liberal society lies in the spread of anti-liberal actions on the back of anti-liberal beliefs. If large numbers of people begin to try to stop their opponents from enjoying the liberal freedoms by closing down their speech and preventing their public association, the operation of liberal society will become impossible at a certain point and authoritarian rule will have to be imposed. Furthermore, if the liberal society is a democracy, the further danger arises that the anti-liberal and anti-democratic parties acquire a majority in the National Assembly, get control of the government and abolish the liberal civil and political freedoms. These actions would be constitutionally valid if the liberal freedoms are not enshrined in a constitution in the form of a basic scheme of human rights, respect for which is required for constitutionally valid actions.

Such a constitution allows a liberal society to defend itself against destruction by anti-liberal parties through a government declared ban on their activities. This would involve a liberal government removing the liberal rights of free speech and association from these parties and might be thought to involve the government in a contradiction. However, as we saw in the discussion of the Brandenburg principle regarding the limits of free speech and association, these freedoms cannot be supposed to be enjoyed without any limits. A liberal society and government must be allowed, like any other such entity, to defend itself from destruction by its enemies. The Brandenburg principle extends the exercise of the liberal freedoms up to the point at which it constitutes an incitement to the commitment of imminent criminal actions. It would not be just to call this an example of liberal hypocrisy: the liberal pretends to offer you freedom, but at the point at which that freedom threatens his existence, he will withdraw it. This is not hypocrisy. The liberal is offering you the greatest amount of equal freedom compatible with the existence of a society in which such equal freedom can be enjoyed. Beyond that, liberal society and the liberal freedoms become unsustainable. No liberal society means no liberal freedoms. The hypocrisy lies with the anti-liberal complainant that his freedom to destroy the freedom of others is being violated.

Nowadays, the anti-liberal forces are more subtle than the fascist parties of the past. They do not seek explicitly to destroy the liberal-democratic freedoms by formally abolishing them. They undermine them and make them inoperative by acquiring control of the media and legal system while preserving the liberal-democratic constitutional forms. This enables them to manipulate the news the people have access to and to pursue their opponents in the courts with trumped-up charges on which the corrupt judges will secure convictions. Add some degree of electoral fraud, constant harassment and outright thuggery and the genuine liberal parties will be stymied. In these respects, the anti-liberal semi-fascist type parties in government, such as Putin's in Russia, have become more like the ruling communist parties that have always pretended to guarantee the rights of their subjects through liberal-sounding constitutions while requiring that the rights must be exercised in a way compatible with the permanent rule of the communist party.

I have argued that a viable liberal society must believe that its members have a sufficient capacity for second level autonomy to be able to critically evaluate anti-liberal attacks on liberal practices and values and critically endorse their liberal system. Furthermore, this capacity must be adequately developed through their education. This may sound absurdly ambitious and implausible. But I do not think it is. The capacity required can be reduced to the following:

1 An ability to understand the basics of autonomy and its two levels. At bottom, this is not a difficult idea. Everybody can reason about what to believe and what to do in particular circumstances and can see that she is, and human beings are, reasoning beings. Everybody can grasp first level autonomy: how to organize her life on the basis of her values. Everybody can grasp the idea of the second level: disputes over values and the possibility of reasoning about them.
2 An ability to understand the practice of an equal freedom: equal religious toleration and its limits is not a difficult idea with which to begin.
3 An ability to understand the difference between a liberal society and an illiberal one in which the freedoms are substantially restricted.
4 An ability to think about the advantages and disadvantages of the two types of society in terms of the values of autonomy and subjection and the different types of well-being.

While these basics involve philosophical ideas, philosophy comes in different degrees of sophistication and nothing very sophisticated is being demanded of liberal citizens. Nevertheless, more is demanded of a liberal citizen than of a Christian in a Christian society or a Muslim in a Muslim society because the liberal society cannot offload its members' capacity for second level autonomy onto an authoritarian elite. It is not that there is no intellectual elite in liberal society, but rather that it has no coercive authority.[3]

In sum, with regard to the essential human value of autonomy, liberal society must count much more highly than illiberal societies because it is organized around giving autonomy a special place.

LIBERALISM AND ASSOCIATIONAL WELL-BEING

This section will raise the question of whether liberalism's emphasis on flourishing through the development of the autonomy of its members does not have serious consequences for the well-being they derive from the enjoyment of strong communal ties. I shall take for granted that having communal ties, being at home in a particular community with its own territory and way of life, is a powerful source of well-being. However, I have argued in the previous chapter that a viable liberal society must have forged a reasonably strong "we" identity among its members which I expanded into the notion of a national identity. So, on this view it cannot be the case that a liberal society destroys all communal ties among its members. Yet, there is a sense in which it is incompatible with a certain type of self-governing community. Returning to the distinction between first and second level autonomy, there can be societies in which second level autonomy is effectively absent for all the members. There is no intellectual elite that engages in reflective evaluation of types of social organization and bestows its authority on the existing form. All the members have an unreflective identification with, and attachment to, their society as what has existed since its foundation in the dim past and can only exist in that form. This is a tribal society organized as a kin-group and having no internal diversity of beliefs and values. Their individual identity is embedded in that of the tribe as an individual member of the X tribe and not as an individual human being with his own individual destiny in the world in principle separate from that of his tribe. In these circumstances, liberalism is irrelevant and makes no sense. Liberalism only becomes a meaningful option for a society once diversity and potential conflicts of beliefs and values have emerged. It is a way of managing these that does not attempt to recreate unity through the coercive imposition of one orthodoxy on all the rest. But it is not liberalism that brings about the diversity. That arises from the evolution and growth of societies. Of course, liberalism encourages it to flourish. So, it is not liberalism that destroys the strong communal ties of the unreflective community. Liberalism is an experiment in maintaining or creating a unity in a community while protecting diversity. If successful, it is obviously superior in terms of the well-being of its members than those attempts to recreate unity by eliminating the differences by force and repression.

It is not the only way of managing a degree of diversity in society. Muslim empires in particular did this by granting particular religious communities rights of self-government in limited respects – their religious affairs and family laws. This self-government was not only limited in respect of spheres of life but also in regard to the religious communities tolerated – the Christian and the Jewish. Furthermore, the members of these communities could not escape their legal identities except by converting to Islam. They obviously did not enjoy individual freedom in the liberal sense. Finally, these communities were subject ones. The members had no political rights and what rights they had were enjoyed only at the whim of the Muslim ruler and his will to protect them from the hostility of Muslim crowds. It should be said that this limited tolerance was far better than the intolerance exercised by the Christian empires towards everybody but the orthodox Christian even if it falls far short of the freedom that liberalism has to offer.

LIBERALISM AND SPIRITUAL WELL-BEING

By spiritual well-being I mean the sense of well-being that may be obtained through beliefs about the relation of the world and its inhabitants, and in particular human beings, to a power that transcends the world and is benevolently disposed towards it, or to a power that is immanent in the world including all its parts as well as us human beings. The main monotheist religions have adopted the transcendent view. This power has created the world and its inhabitants for a purpose, and if human beings conduct themselves in accordance with the divine plan, they will be incorporated in some sort of eternal being. Since individual human lives, and indeed the collective lives of societies, are extremely vulnerable to destruction through human accidents and vices, natural or man-made disasters, disease, the hostility of other human beings and finally old age, these stories about the meaning of human life from the perspective of universal being can bring relief to individuals fearfully aware of their own contingency and fragility. Furthermore, since these religions usually come with an appended moral code of behaviour, they claim to give the stamp of God's authority to what may otherwise be seen as human inventions that are open to challenge and transformation.

These ideas are relevant to the question of liberalism because it is often criticized and rejected by the religious on the grounds that it is an essentially secular system of beliefs and hence has no other ground than human will. This is, in particular, the standard critique of liberal-democracy of Muslim divines. Religious authorities, indeed, have an obvious self-interest in making such claims since their own positions depend on their unprovable assertions to know God's mind on these issues. But the criticism is false. There is nothing in either the history of liberalism or in the account of it that has been given in this book that precludes grounding liberalism in beliefs about God. However, those liberal-compatible religious beliefs have a problem with the appeal to sacred texts which are supposed to tell human beings how to live. From a liberal point of view, all we have to go on in order to discover how to live are the facts about God's creation. He has created the world and all the creatures in it including human beings. This creation might have come about through the immediate coming into existence of the different species or through a process of evolution that he has set in train. However we envisage this creation, the facts are that there exist different species now, including human beings. These species have particular natures which are what they are because of God's will that they should be so. In particular, he has willed that human beings are rational social animals. Since he has created us with this nature, he must want us to live by exercising the powers that he has willed for us. The full exercise of these powers in the members of a society can only be achieved by organizing society along liberal-democratic lines. This, then, is how God wants human beings to live. We can know that this is his will because we can work out through the exercise of the powers that he has willed for us that a liberal-democratic society is the most fulfilling for beings with our nature.

This sort of religious belief is compatible with sacred text-based religion only if the texts can be interpreted to endorse the liberal values. So, it tends to reject revealed religion for natural religion – a religion based on what the natural operations of the human mind can reasonably establish about God and his creation. A religious-based liberalism of this kind should arrive at the same answer to the question of how human beings should live as one that has proceeded without reference to God, as has the account of liberalism in this book until this section. So, perhaps the religious critics of secular liberalism are correct in their claim that liberalism must rest the authority of its ethical order on human will. For natural religion has nothing else to go on in its ethical theorizing than human nature understood as rational social animal, which is all that confronts the secular liberal also. Yet, the same is true of those human beings who claim to have direct access to God's mind through the possession of sacred texts. If there is one thing that is certain in these matters, it is that God could not have created us with the rational powers that he has and at the same time willed that we slavishly and uncritically follow the dictates of texts produced by human beings thousands of years ago who assert that God speaks through them. To believe that is an insult to God's intelligence.

FURTHER READING

The classic work on the dangers in the rise of the meritocracy is M. Young (1958).

The claim that the degree of inequality in a society seriously affects the general well-being is powerfully argued by Wilkinson and Pickett (2009).

On the notion of well-being, see Griffin (1986), Sumner (1996) and Crisp (2013).

NOTES

1 Rousseau (1964). What Rousseau actually said was "Finally, I would prove that if one sees a handful of powerful and rich men at the height of grandeur and fortune, while the crowd grovels in obscurity and misery, it is because the former prize the things they enjoy only insofar as the others are deprived of them; and because, without changing their condition, they would cease to be happy if the people ceased to be miserable". *Discourse on the Origins of Inequality*, p.175.
2 Of course, men did not first adopt this view of women and then impose patriarchy on them. The view rationalizes their drive for domination.
3 This claim needs qualification. The liberal government, including the legislative branch, must enact and enforce the rules elaborating the liberal way of life and must insist on the teaching of liberal values and practices in its educational institutions. Yet, the liberal government has no authority to coerce people into believing in liberalism.

PART III

LIBERAL THEORIES

INTRODUCTION

The major task of an adequate liberal theory is to give an account of why human beings should adopt a liberal organization of their society rather than some other way of living together. There are two broad approaches to this task. One attempts to show that liberal forms of living together are the only ones that meet the fundamental requirements of ethics. In other words there is no ethical alternative. The second allows that there are various ways of meeting the fundamental ethical requirements but that liberal forms of collective life are better than any known alternative.

Either way the theory has to provide also an interpretation of freedom and equality that resolves the disputes about these concepts discussed in Part II. An adequate theory will show as well why a coercive state is a necessary aspect of liberal organization and why such considerations involve a multi-state world with its attendant problems or, in the case of libertarian anarchism, it must provide good reasons for thinking that no state could satisfy the ethical requirements. Finally, it would seem that some account should be given of the consequences of liberalism for the well-being of those living under liberal forms. However, if your theory is of the first type mentioned here, in which the claim is made that only liberal principles satisfy the fundamental ethical requirements, you will think that the question of well-being is ethically irrelevant. The only well-being an ethical agent is entitled to is one that is compatible with her respect for ethical laws.

In the final part of the book I shall discuss, first, libertarian theories grounded in the idea of a natural right to liberty and focusing on the 20th-century theorist Robert Nozick and the 17th-century writer John Locke. I shall then switch my attention to the classical utilitarians, J. Bentham and J.S. Mill, who seek to show that we should adopt liberal forms because that will result in the attainment of the greatest amount of happiness. The next chapter will sketch the liberal theory of the radically anti-utilitarian and enormously influential 18th-century ethical theorist, Immanuel Kant, before turning to the late 20th-century liberal theorists who have done so much to revive serious philosophizing about ethics and politics – John Rawls, Ronald Dworkin and Joseph Raz. The book finishes with my own attempt to deal with the inadequacies I will have identified in the above theories.

The development of political theories of a recognizably liberal character occurred in Northern Europe in the 17th century by thinkers who were Christians of Protestant persuasion. The main figures were Hugo Grotius in the Netherlands, Thomas Hobbes and John Locke in England, and Samuel Pufendorf in Germany. The tradition of thought they established is variously called the modern natural law doctrine or the theory of natural rights and social contract. The main novel feature of this doctrine is the attempt to construct a conception of a legitimate social and political order from minimalist assumptions about individuals' rights in a state of nature. The state of nature is a state of the world in which independent individuals interact without the constraints or support of a coercively organized society. Such individuals, it is assumed, will be primarily motivated to preserve themselves by seeking to protect their lives, liberties and possessions from invasion by others. Because of the insecurity of such a state, they will be driven to come to an agreement to create a political society with the right to establish and enforce common laws. The theorists mentioned differ among themselves over the details of this construction, and Thomas Hobbes is a notorious outlying thinker in the tradition.

The liberal character of the doctrine is contained in the foundational idea of a natural right to liberty restricted only by the duty to respect the equal rights of others. Each individual exercises his natural liberty by deciding for himself how best to preserve himself. Thus, no one is naturally subject to another, and the socio-political order must be grounded in each person's will to enter together with the others into a political society. Furthermore, the laws of political society must establish only equal constraints on natural liberty and restrict liberty no more than is necessary to achieve security and order for members to go about their private business.

A striking feature of the Europe in which this modern natural law doctrine developed was the devastating religious conflict between Protestants and Catholics. This conflict was carried on through a good part of the 16th and 17th centuries and came to a head in the 30 Years' War of 1618–48 which was fought mainly on the territories of the German states but involved armies from Sweden, France, Denmark, the Netherlands and Spain as well. The horrendous massacres of Christians by other Christians that were carried out throughout this period led to the emergence of strong pressure on the main parties to accept the practice of mutual tolerance. The modern law theorists were part of the intellectual movement for tolerance. While remaining believers in the Christian God, they developed a minimalist version of Christian doctrine that they believed all Christians could endorse. They all think of the world and its creatures as created by God and believe that the natural laws they have worked out through the exercise of their God-given natural rational powers are morally obligatory on human beings because that obligation is grounded in God's will or reason. While they appeal to the Christian texts to support their view, they do not believe that human beings can know what God's purpose is in creating the world and human beings. All that we can know is that Jesus is the saviour and that the laws we should follow in our mutual relations are those that they have worked out in their natural law doctrine.

However, radical religious conflict is not the only feature of contemporary Europe that helps us to understand the success of the new proto-liberal doctrine. Significant economic and political developments contributed to its reception. The economic events consist in the emergence of a capitalist merchant class that is independent of both the feudal nobility and the restrictive trade practices of the guild-dominated and self-governing towns. The interests of this class in economic freedom coincided to some degree with the interests of monarchs who were trying to liberate their control of their territories from the internal restrictions arising from the traditional powers of the feudal nobility and self-governing towns, and from the external constraints contained in the spiritual and material overlordship of Catholic Pope and Holy Roman Emperor. The modern sovereign state that came into existence in this period by asserting and vindicating its absolute political right over its territory and inhabitants, found itself driven to pursue the increase of its power and wealth vis-à-vis other such states by adopting mercantilist economic policies in alliance with the new capitalist class.

A certain affinity can be seen to exist also between the self-understanding of the modern sovereign state and the new natural law doctrine. For both there exists no intermediate groups between the absolute state and the individual subject that have any claims to limit the state's inherent authority. On the one hand, there is the state and, on the other, the collection of individuals who are bound together through their equal subjection to the political society. The natural rights doctrine does, indeed, give individuals rights which in the theory of Locke are supposed to protect them from the exercise of arbitrary power by rulers. But this notoriously creates problems for the coherence of his theory, since at the same time he endorses the absolute sovereignty of the political society over its members.

Natural rights principles became the ideological basis of the American and French Revolutions at the end of the 18th century. Yet, at the same time the doctrine was being subject to vigorous challenge by liberal-inclined thinkers, especially in Great Britain. These were the Utilitarians led by Jeremy Bentham. The Utilitarians entirely rejected the modern natural law doctrine's individualist fantasy of a state of nature in which individuals enjoyed rights, and instead claimed to derive the liberal policies from calculations of what social arrangements would maximize the general happiness. While in Germany in the thought of Kant and Hegel, the liberal ideas are historicized as a story about the development of reason in history.

If I, subsequently, leap forward in time from a discussion of Kant's thought to the liberal theories of John Rawls and the post-Rawlsians of the 1970s and 1980s, it is because nothing radically new in liberal theory was produced in that period. There took place, indeed, a slow decline, accelerated after WWI, into a widespread scepticism about the possibility of philosophical theorizing in ethics and politics. The significance of Rawls lies in the widely held belief that he had found a way of resuscitating the activity of philosophical reasoning about ethics and politics and of giving such reasoning a liberal content. Whether this belief is correct or not, it has certainly led to an outburst of political theorizing in the English-speaking academies.

FURTHER READING

A classic essay on the prevailing scepticism in this period is to be found in Berlin's essay, "Does Political Theory Still Exist?" (1978).

The essay was in fact first published in French in 1961.

An example of the reduced ambitions of political theory at this time is Weldon (1953).

LIBERTARIAN THEORIES

A NATURAL RIGHT TO LIBERTY

Libertarian thinkers argue that only a coercive state with minimal functions can be ethically justified. In the case of the libertarian anarchists, no state at all can be so justified. The minimal state conclusion might be the result of a utilitarian argument about the consequences for the general happiness of the state taking on different functions. I shall touch on such an argument in the next chapter. Here I shall concentrate on minimal state theories that rest on the claim to a natural right to liberty. The idea of a natural right to liberty as the foundational principle of social and political order is the idea that the only legitimate restriction on my doing what I please is the requirement to respect the equal right to liberty of other human beings. Otherwise, I am bound only by what I can agree to in my own interest. This might include a minimal state or it might not.

If I have a natural right to liberty and there is nothing that distinguishes me as a human being from everyone else, then I must acknowledge an equal natural right to liberty in them. But why does anyone have such a right? Robert Nozick (1938–2002) believes that the best account of the ground of such a right is probably that human beings have the capacity for autonomy and there is something inherently worthy of respect about a being with the capacity for autonomy.[1] So we must not invade its liberty.

Robert Nozick was a US philosopher working at Harvard University at the same time as John Rawls. He was clearly motivated to refute the egalitarianism of Rawls's theory. His appeal to everyone's natural right to exercise their liberty in an initially fair position enables him to reject the egalitarian's overriding of individual liberty by the requirement to maintain equal outcomes or inputs. John Locke (1632–1704), whom we have already met earlier, arrives at an equal liberty by first claiming that we are all the property of God because he made us and sent us into the world "to last during his, not one another's, pleasure".[2] So we are not licensed by God to destroy others whenever we want. But this argument doesn't show that our natural liberty is an equal one. Since God gave us unequal rational abilities, he might have intended that the more rational should rule. Locke's second claim is that if God had wanted us to enjoy an unequal liberty, he would have made this clear in some way. In the absence of such directions from God, it is evident, he says that "creatures of the same species and rank, promiscuously born to all the same advantages of nature and the use of the same faculties, should also be equal one amongst another without subordination or subjection".[3] This hardly deals with the suggested objection that unequal natural rational abilities could be such a sign from God. It begs that question.

Whatever the weaknesses in their arguments for an equality of liberty, it is very clear that this is indeed how they move from the individual's right to his natural liberty to the construction of a liberal order. Natural liberty is the right not to be subject to the will of another without one's consent. If everyone has the same right, no one may force another against his will to agree to something or use fraud to deceive him into an agreement that he would not have consented to without the deceit. All relations must be consensual. Exception is, of course, made for acts of self-defence or for securing redress for an injury to one's person or property by another.

A major problem in this type of theory is how one can acquire rights in things. If one's natural right to liberty is to mean anything, it must be possible to have a right to move around and use some parts of the earth's surface without obtaining the prior agreement of all other human beings. To obtain such agreement would not be possible, and so one's natural right to liberty could not be actualized in the external world. The standard answer is to appeal to a right of the first occupant. In the state of nature we must suppose that originally there were few people and much unoccupied land and resources. So, in occupying unoccupied parts of the earth's surface and using its unused resources, one is violating no one else's liberty to occupy some other part of the world. Such acquisition embodies one's natural liberty in things, and others must respect that property because in it lies one's rightful will. But what is supposed to happen when all the world is occupied and no resources are left for latecomers to take into their possession? For Locke there are two initial constraints on rightful acquisition: first, one is only entitled to appropriate enough to satisfy what one needs to preserve oneself. Second, one must leave enough and as good of whatever one appropriates for others.[4] So, one cannot appropriate the only water supply in an area and leave all the others to die of thirst. Furthermore, one rightfully appropriates some unowned thing only through the work of one's hands or the labour of one's body (or that of one's servant). Nozick adopts the second of these Lockean constraints. But he interprets it to mean that latecomers are entitled to have access to the level of resources they could have obtained through their own labour on unoccupied territory in an original state of nature. So, if there is no supply of water left for them to access, they are entitled to free access to other people's water for the satisfaction of the needs they would have been able to satisfy when unappropriated water still existed.[5] In general a latecomer in the contemporary capitalist United States is entitled to have access to a standard of living that he could have reached through his own labour on unoccupied resources in an original state of nature. Nozick believes that this would not have been very high and is easily met by an ordinary employee in the contemporary capitalist economy.

Locke evades his constraint on legitimate appropriation arising from having to leave enough and as good for others in a similar way to Nozick. He appeals to the enormous productivity of an economy which allows capital accumulation with the result that a mere day labourer in England lives better than a King among the Native American Indian tribes.[6] The other constraint is lifted by the agreement to the introduction of money. This allows people to accumulate wealth without limit. Since money works only through everyone's agreement to treat it as a store of value and medium of exchange, everyone can be taken to have agreed to the consequences of money in the unequal distribution of wealth.

THE STATE

So far, no mention has been made of a state. The minimal functions of a state are to make and enforce rules of interaction for the inhabitants of the territory it controls and to protect them from invasion from outside. A state necessarily has the right to use force to compel the inhabitants of its territory to comply with its rules, and this includes the right to apprehend and punish those who do not comply. Since the state's inhabitants have to obey the rules on threat of punishment whether or not they have agreed to them, it looks as though the state is necessarily in potential violation of their natural liberty and in actual violation whenever they do not like the rule they are forced to obey. Locke's answer to this problem is the contract theory of the state. Because of the inconveniences of the state of nature, the inhabitants of an area will get together and bind themselves to create and support a political association that has these stated functions and rights. Thus, the state violates no one's natural liberty because all have consented to its rule, including the use of force against themselves should they break the rules.

However, the government of a state is legitimate, and the rules it enacts have to be obeyed only if they conform to the laws of nature. These are the elaboration of the principle of an equal liberty as applied to the interactions of the state's subjects. If the government through its legislation and policies violates these laws and hence the rights of its subjects, it is in rebellion against them and may be opposed by the people as they think fit. The inconveniences of the state of nature that the invention of the state is supposed to remedy arise from two basic causes: first, the fact that everyone in that state is judge and enforcer of the laws of nature in his own case and will naturally interpret the law to suit himself. Second, besides the natural lawlessness of a minority of human beings, most people are no great observers of the law if they can get away with non-compliance. The remedy is the creation of an impartial and authoritative judge and effective enforcer. This is the state in its minimal functions.[7]

According to the contract theory of political obligation, the state in its minimal functions does not violate our natural liberty because we have exercised our natural liberty in consenting to its creation. But even if in the first instance such a contract took place, subsequent generations could not be bound by it since they will not have consented. Locke has two suggestions as to how their consent may be presupposed. On the first, if someone inherits property in the territory of the state, by entering into his rights he tacitly consents to the authority of the political society into whose territory that property has been incorporated by the initial contract. On the second, anyone resident in, or passing through, a state's territory and thereby enjoying the rule of law that the state provides is ipso facto bound to accept its authority. However, Locke recognizes that consent to a government in these ways does not make a person a full member of that society. Nothing but an express promise or compact will do.[8] If so, the subsequent generations born into a state already in existence could not have the full obligations of members to that state unless they had actually consented to it. Since, as far as I am aware, they are nowhere required to make such commitments, nobody is subject to full political obligation on the Lockean theory.

In fact, the only remotely plausible form of the contract theory of the state is that of rational consent. According to this view, given that the only alternative to the coercive state is the chaos of the state of nature, it would be rational for everyone faced with this choice to bind herself to create and maintain a state. All human beings can understand this reasoning. Hence, so long as a state follows the natural law constraints on its operations, anyone residing in such a state can be taken to have consented to its authority whether or not they have actually done so. But rational consent is not actual consent and cannot really be called consent at all. It describes only what every rational person would do in her own interest.

Nozick deals with these problems somewhat differently. He imagines that in the state of nature among the services that some enterprises will offer for sale to people will be the adjudication of claims of loss or injury perpetrated by others as well as protection from aggression by others. Nozick envisages that a dominant protective association will emerge in different geographical areas through a process which does not violate anyone's natural liberty. As one association becomes more successful in attracting clients in its area through its ability to get better results for them, the incentive for the remaining inhabitants of the area to transfer their custom to the dominant association can only grow until it acquires a de facto monopoly in that area. Such a dominant protective association will still not be a state as standardly understood if it does not force all inhabitants in its area to be its clients. If it allows independents to operate by exercising their natural rights to interpret and enforce the laws of nature themselves, no one's rights will have been violated. Its own clients will be obliged by the association's rules and procedures only because they have agreed to take out protection policies with it. However, Nozick believes that the dominant protective association should, in the interests of protecting its existing clients from being exposed to the risky procedures of the independents, ban the independents and compensate them for that loss by providing them freely with its own protection. Thereby, a minimal state has, supposedly, come into existence without the violation of anyone's rights.[9]

On the face of it, banning the independents is violating their natural rights. Nozick's claim to the contrary depends on his view that the dominant protective association has a right to forcibly prevent anyone from using risky procedures of adjudicating and enforcing the laws of nature on its clients. This claim is very doubtful. What anyone in the state of nature has a right to do in the face of someone using risky procedures in interpreting and enforcing the law of nature is to take what measures he thinks fit to protect himself. But among such measures cannot be the right to extinguish another's right. Since the dominant association's rights are only the sum of its clients' rights, it cannot acquire a right that they didn't have. I conclude that a dominant protective association cannot become a state claiming coercive authority over everyone in its geographical area without violating the independents' natural liberty. In that case, if neither Locke's nor Nozick's justification of the minimal state nor any similar justification is valid, anarchism would have to be the appropriate conclusion for a libertarian to arrive at.

THE IDEA OF A STATE OF NATURE AND THE INADEQUACY OF LIBERTARIANISM

In the construction of a libertarian theory, the idea of a state of nature plays a seemingly essential role. Yet, it appears to be so absurd as to damn the theory from the outset. Of course human beings did not first emerge as independents but as members of small groups with close emotional and normative ties having little to do with a natural right to liberty. While the early modern political theorists, including Locke, who used the idea appear to have believed in its real existence, perhaps we can treat it as a hypothesis based on the capacity for autonomy of developed human beings. So we start with human beings living in, and being formed by, collectivities with their own authoritatively enforced norms of conduct as they always have. Nevertheless, the theorist has to attribute to these human beings a capacity for autonomy at the second level. That is to say, they can stand back from their immersion in their society's norms and values and can reflectively evaluate them from the perspective of the nature and interests of the human beings who are its members. These members know themselves to have the capacity for autonomy and believe, with Nozick, that its possession establishes an inherent worthiness in its bearer, such that the bearer is entitled to a natural right to liberty and cannot rightly be subject to another without his own consent. In order to arrive at an understanding of the social arrangements that autonomous persons possessing a natural right to liberty could agree to, we have to begin by positing a state of nature in which there is no social authority or coercive norms but only independents with the minimal duty to respect the equal liberty of others and the right to interpret and enforce this requirement for themselves. In other words, we arrive at an account of just social and political arrangements from the hypothesis of independent individuals exercising their natural right to liberty in a state of nature, and this right is derived from the inherent worthiness of beings with the capacity for autonomy.

The trouble with this hypothesis, however, remains that the whole social background of the actual human being is assumed away, and it appears that individuals can make rational choices in their best interests without the need for such a background. In those circumstances, when they come to agree to form a collectivity with the right to enforce its rules on its members, these independents will opt for a minimal state. The hypothesis makes them unaware that they would not enjoy the developed capacity to make rational choices at all unless they had first been formed in a collectivity which, through its beliefs and values, taught its members how to reason about how to live and what to believe. If we bring this background back in, then we must accept that the so-called independents are actually and unavoidably members of some collectivity and that the second level autonomy that they have arrived at only enables them to reflect on and propose alternatives to their existing collective arrangements. The supposed proposal of an arrangement based on the possession by each of a natural right to liberty must be ruled out as incompatible with the recognition of that background collectivity. Any acceptable proposal must be evaluated on the basis that it constitutes a rule for the members' interactions. It will thus presuppose the existence of the collectivity that the hypothesis of a natural right to liberty denies. The only way in which the idea of a social order based on an equal liberty could be entertained, then, would be by proposing such a principle to operate within the context of the fundamental needs of an independent political society concerned with its security and prosperity and possessing a sufficiently strong "we" identity to maintain itself over time. The operation of the principle of equal liberty would, thus, necessarily be limited by such needs. This is what I have been attempting to do in the first two Parts of this work.

Trying to elaborate the idea of a social order based on a natural right to liberty, naturally leads, as I claimed earlier, to the idea of a minimal state. This is because by removing the social background of individual life, it is assumed that fully developed adults enjoying a natural right to liberty can be trusted to enter into only those agreements that are in their interest. So, if the starting point for all is fair, then the result of uncoerced and undeceived choices by persons exercising their natural right will be just, and no one will have any ground to complain about the inequalities that will result. Nozick expresses his idea of justice in the following terms: from each as they choose to each as they are chosen.[10]

Actually, an element of redistribution is likely to exist in the Nozickian state. Latecomers, who find that there are no unowned resources left for them to appropriate, are entitled to access resources up to the level they would have been able to attain in the original state of nature before everything was appropriated. If they cannot reach this level by finding employment in the capitalist economy, the state would have to tax those with a surplus of resources to provide for them. Otherwise, since no one has any grounds to complain that his rights have been violated by the system of free exchange, the only defensible function of the state, if there is any at all, is the protection of people's rights to liberty from violation by insiders or outsiders of one's society.

What this ignores is that the good in liberty does not lie in itself but in the control it allows one to have over one's life, and this value increases as the control over one's life is extended. Thus, if one's only choices are which bridge to seek shelter under for the night or where to scavenge for food the next day, the degree of one's control will be very limited, and the formal liberty one has to do many other things which yet one is not in a position to do will be worthless. As the level of one's access to resources and the number and quality of one's options increases, so will the worth of liberty to that person. The equal possession of the rights to liberty does not mean that the worth of those rights to different people will be equal. On Nozick's own view, a person is entitled to a natural right to liberty because of his inherent worthiness as a being capable of autonomy. But if autonomy comes in degrees and is dependent on the level of his resources and options as well as his formal liberties, enormous inequalities in the worth to people of their liberties might not be acceptable from the point of view of their equal worth as autonomous beings. At least some threshold level of access to resources and availability of options would seem to be required. This will be even more evident if we bring back the social context in which, alone, people can develop their capacities for autonomy. In such a context, a person must be valued as an equal member of society who together with the others grounds the "we" identity that must be presupposed in a meaningful discussion of equal liberties. Such an equal citizen cannot be a destitute and uneducated scavenger living from day to day. He must have enjoyed reasonable formative and educational conditions, and access to a threshold level of resources and options, if he is going to be able to respect others and be respected as an equal citizen.

A final comment on the libertarian theory: in terms of its conception of a just social and political order grounded in autonomous individuals who are inherently entitled to a natural right to liberty, there is no alternative that would have any degree of moral worth.

Any putative alternative would violate the natural right to liberty. Thus there would be no point in considering the implications of this order for the well-being of its subjects, since the subjects would not be morally entitled to the possible fruits of a different order.

FURTHER READING

Locke (1964) and Nozick (1974).
On Locke, read the excellent Lloyd Thomas (1995). Also Hampsher-Monk (1992).
On Nozick, read Wolff (1991).
On libertarianism in general, see Vallentyne (2002).

NOTES

1 Nozick (1974, pp.49–51).
2 Locke (1964) 2nd Treatise, para 6.
3 Ibid. para 4.
4 Ibid. paras 31–3.
5 Nozick (1974, pp.162–72).
6 Locke (1864) para 41.
7 Ibid., Chap. 9.
8 Ibid., paras 120–2.
9 Nozick (1974, Chap. 2).
10 Ibid., p.160.

UTILITARIAN THEORIES OF LIBERALISM

THE PRINCIPLE OF UTILITY

The primary British utilitarians are Jeremy Bentham and John Stuart Mill. They were extraordinarily successful in the UK in promoting the utilitarian doctrine as an ethical alternative to the theory of natural rights and the social contract. The principle of utility holds that an action is right if it will produce a greater amount of utility than any alternative and wrong if the contrary holds. Since one cannot know exactly what the consequences of actions will be, one must rely on probabilistic calculations. By utility the original theorists meant happiness, and by happiness they meant pleasure and the absence of pain. So, right actions will be ones that maximize the net amount of pleasure produced. However, Mill was very generous in what he thought could be included in that end. Anything that is, at first, only a means to pleasure can through a psychological process become part of the end. Thus accumulating money is a means to pleasure because of the uses to which money can be put. But the miser comes to love the money for its own sake and gets pleasure from merely possessing it. Mill believes that virtue and individuality can and should be desired for their own sake and thus become part of the end that people pursue. Obviously, he does not think that money should have this status. Furthermore, one can include in the idea of utility anything that one thinks is a good in itself. So if one believes that autonomy is a good in itself, one can adopt the consequential structure of utilitarian thinking and hold that right actions are those that maximize the actualization of autonomy. Utilitarianism is in this respect a maximizing or totalizing doctrine. Individuals and actions are good or bad depending on their contribution to a total amount of something. This contrasts with ethical doctrines that attach value to individuals in themselves. On such a view individuals may have rights quite independently of their contribution to a total and you are not entitled to violate those rights in order to increase the total. The pursuit of the good is subject to the constraint of a principle. One example would be a natural right to liberty.

SECONDARY PRINCIPLES

The above section describes the structure of utilitarian thinking as though the utilitarian agent had to calculate the probable consequences of his act at the point at which he is contemplating action. This view is variously called act utilitarianism or direct utilitarianism. An alternative view requires that the principle of utility be applied not to acts but to rules or practices which, if generally followed, produce the most utility. Quite apart from the difficulty of calculating the consequences of particular acts, act or direct utilitarianism is held to ignore threshold effects. For instance, one act of crossing a lawn may have no deleterious consequence for the state of the lawn. If I cross it and no one else does, the lawn crossing will save me time, give me pleasure and have no bad effects. The same may apply to some subsequent lawn crossings. But beyond a certain point, any further lawn crossings start to produce a deterioration in the lawn. If I calculate the effect of my lawn crossing as part of a general practice of lawn crossing in that place rather than as a single act, then the consequences of my act will be very much worse, and it will be obvious that I should not cross the lawn. Since human beings engage in coordinated practices, such as following rules not to cross lawn X, it is surely the consequences of following this or that rule that we should be trying to calculate from a utilitarian point of view.

Yet, if we possessed perfect information regarding the effect of lawn crossings, we would see that even when the general practice of not crossing the lawn was in place, there would be some number of lawn-crossings which, because they fell below the threshold, would increase the total happiness. Since utilitarianism directs us to seek to maximize the total happiness, this combination of rule and exemptions would be prescribed. But we do not actually possess perfect information about the consequences of such combinations of rules and exemptions. Furthermore, human beings are known to be very imperfect moral beings. So, if they are morally required to follow certain rules only when exemption from the rule would not increase the total happiness, there is very likely to be a vast excess of self-permitted exemptions above the level that an ideal utilitarian calculator with perfect information would allow. In these less than ideal circumstances in which the utilitarian calculus has to be applied, it makes sense for human beings to bind themselves to follow secondary rules or practices. In other words those rules or practices which, if generally followed, would produce more happiness than any alternative set of such rules. But in order to ensure that these practices are generally followed, we may have to believe that we must follow them without regard to the consequences.

R.M. Hare has developed this idea at length, distinguishing the two levels of utilitarian thinking into proletarian and archangelic types. Our ordinary moral thinking – when we tell each other not to kill, steal, lie, defraud and so on without regard to the consequences – is, nevertheless, based on the idea of secondary principles that if generally followed will maximize happiness given that human beings are not ideal utilitarian agents. This is proletarian moral thinking because it is the level that ordinary human beings are capable of grasping and following most of the time. But we are also capable of reflecting on our practices from the perspective of a well-informed and benevolent ideal utilitarian agent and judging whether our ordinary moral practices need adjustment or indeed radical change. This is the perspective of the utilitarian archangel. The point of this division of our moral labour is to prevent the utilitarian doctrine from implausibly requiring everybody to try to be a perfect utilitarian calculator all the time. Whether this division works or not I shall consider after discussing Bentham's appeal to secondary principles.

UTILITARIAN LIBERALISM: JEREMY BENTHAM (1748–1832)

Utilitarianism's concern with maximizing happiness or some other conception of the ultimate good for human and other sentient beings easily lends itself to anti-liberal paternalist moral thinking. If one could promote the general welfare by direct government action, utilitarianism would embrace the possibility with enthusiasm. So, for utilitarians to support liberal practices, they must believe that for a society to adopt these practices and follow them broadly without regard to the consequences will produce the best consequences. The major utilitarians of the 19th century did believe this. Jeremy Bentham believed that the best way for governments to maximize the general happiness was through laws which protected each person's liberty to pursue his own happiness as he thought best provided that he did not cause pain to others. He believed this because, although he thought that it was in principle possible to quantify the total amount of happiness summed over different people, he accepted that in practice this would be very difficult. Instead, then, of giving some utilitarian bureaucrat the impossible duty of distributing sources of pleasure and pain with the aim of maximizing the total of net pleasure, he thought that it would be better to let each person decide for himself what gave him pleasure. That person was the one with the strongest motive to get the decision right for himself and with the best knowledge of his own preferences.[1] Nevertheless, governments had to limit individuals' liberty by laws protecting others from pain and so had to be in a position to establish for themselves the major causes of pain.

Individual negative liberty, then, was a major secondary principle for Bentham. It was not, of course, a natural or human right fundamental to the identification of a just social and political order in the manner of the libertarians of the last chapter. Governments for Bentham had to promote liberty, but they also had to recognize four other major secondary principles. These were subsistence, abundance, security and equality, and they could take precedence over the pursuit of liberty.[2] Subsistence meant the possession of those things the absence of which would cause physical suffering; abundance was the multiplication of the means of happiness; security involved primarily the protection of persons' expectations, threats to which Bentham considered to be a great source of unhappiness. By equality Bentham meant equality of income and wealth. He believed that, other things being equal, an equal distribution of income and wealth would be more likely to maximize happiness than an unequal one. This was because of the diminishing marginal utility of units of wealth: adding one unit of wealth to a poor man will increase his happiness more than the same unit given to a rich man.[3] So, in distributing units of money between people in the first instance, the more equal distribution is more likely to maximize happiness. Of course, it does not follow that taking wealth from the rich man and giving it to the poor will increase the total happiness because of the security and abundance principles. The security of the rich will be substantially undermined by such policies and be a major cause of unhappiness. Furthermore, such policies may reduce the incentive for economic actors to increase their wealth while contributing to the general abundance.

Utilitarianism is a universalist ethic in the sense that it tells ethical agents to maximize the general happiness summed over all human beings at least and usually over all sentient beings. The appropriate political realization of this ethic would then seem to be a world state seeking to maximize happiness for the world's population. However, utilitarians standardly argue for or assume that the political organization of the world into smaller units will do better from a utilitarian point of view than attempts to create and run a world state. Just as, on the liberty principle, the world will go better if individuals possess the liberty to pursue their own good in the way they choose rather than have a government decide for them what gives them happiness. Similarly, the care and upbringing of children will go better if it is allocated to their parents rather than organized through state nurseries. So, maximizing happiness over separate political units whose boundaries follow ethnic or cultural affinities will be a better way to maximize the total happiness in the world rather than attempting to achieve this directly through a world government.

A government constructing its public policy on the basis of Bentham's five principles will have considerable flexibility in judging what combination of these principles, in the situation it finds itself in, will maximize the general happiness. While the liberty principle, of course, supports the adoption of the liberal practices, subsistence is a paternalist welfare principle limiting the liberty of the taxpayers in respect of their use of their wealth. Security is a potentially very conservative principle opposed to changes in the laws that destroy people's expectations. Security considerations conflict with equality ones, and Bentham on the whole gives precedence to security over equality. The abundance principle would seem to favour both individual economic liberty and government economic action to the extent that these policies promote economic growth.

Bentham's secondary principles identify the tendencies of different policies to promote or detract from the general happiness. They do not establish any fundamental rights for individuals. Although his appeal to some of these principles involves his endorsement of liberal practices, nevertheless, the practices may be limited or their values overridden by non-liberal or illiberal considerations depending on what combination of secondary principles is judged most likely to maximize the general happiness. In this respect, the utilitarian theory is standardly criticized by other ethical theorists for allowing the possibility of sacrificing the happiness of some individuals for the sake of increasing the total amount of happiness overall. If the exploitation of a slave or underclass of workers increased the total amount of happiness, the utilitarian theory would recommend it. This is because its fundamental principle is a totalizing one without regard to distributive considerations. From the point of view of the totalizing principle, the distinction between one person and another is of no consequence. A pain to one person can be compensated for by a greater amount of net pleasure to another. The libertarian theory of natural right rejects that idea as do most other ethical theories. There are certain things that it is forbidden to do to a person whatever the consequences.

Can utilitarianism be rescued from this kind of criticism by its formulation in the indirect form discussed in the previous section? The idea is that we should either completely or for most of our lives acquire the disposition to follow certain principles without regard to the consequences. If we do this and the principles are right, we will produce the best consequences. This idea does not involve denying that the principles may sometimes or frequently conflict. When they do, however, we, as proletarians, do not try to calculate what arrangement will produce the largest total of net happiness.

Rather, we judge that, in the circumstances, principle X is of greater inherent importance than principle Y and overrides it. For example, acting to save a life that results in us reneging on a lunch engagement. Yet, utilitarianism tells us as ethical agents that the ground of ethics is the greatest happiness principle. As ethical agents we cannot but ultimately be motivated by this principle and so, it would seem, must always consider overriding our tendency to proletarian moral thinking by the totalizing perspective of the archangel.

UTILITARIAN LIBERALISM: JOHN STUART MILL (1806–1873)

MILL ON LIBERTY

Mill was brought up by his father, who was a disciple of Bentham, to believe in the truth of the utilitarian doctrine. He remained throughout his writing career an adherent of this theory but is generally thought to have refined or modified the doctrine. Mill is also a great hero of liberalism. In particular, his essay "On Liberty" is universally regarded as a classic of liberal thought. However, I am concerned with it here, not so much for the details of his argument but from the point of view of the utilitarian theory that Mill claims supports it.

Mill's defence of liberty rests on what Mill calls "one very simple principle as entitled to govern absolutely the dealings of society with the individual by way of compulsion and control". This principle says that "the sole end for which mankind are warranted, individually or collectively, in interfering with the liberty of action of any of their number is self-protection".[4] Power may be legitimately exercised over a person against his will only to prevent harm to others. He makes a fundamental distinction between self-regarding and other-regarding actions and claims that in regard to the former, a person's "independence is, of right, absolute".[5] I have to say that this last distinction is hopeless. One cannot identify an area of protected liberty for the individual by appealing to actions that are inherently his concern, because what is his concern and not the concern of others depends on the rights to liberty that one believes he possesses. Mill has got the argument the wrong way round. He purports to derive the right to liberty from the existence of self-regarding actions, whereas one has first to establish a right to liberty before one can identify what are legitimately a person's self-regarding concerns and thus what are not the concern of others without his permission.

Mill's confusions on this point have to do no doubt with his desire not to be claiming that his defence of liberty rests on the assertion of a natural right to liberty rather than the utilitarian principle he believes is the ground of ethics. His assertion that the liberty expressed in his very simple principle is an absolute right also strongly suggests that he has in mind but cannot clearly admit such a natural right to liberty. Mill is aware of the difficulty he might be in for he denies explicitly that his argument rests on the assertion of an "abstract right, as a thing independent of utility". Instead, he claims that his principle rests on "utility as the ultimate appeal in all ethical questions". However, "it must be utility in the largest sense grounded on the permanent interests of a man as a progressive being".[6] The only way to make sense of Mill's ideas here is to drop the distinction between self-regarding and other-regarding actions. We can also say that Mill is asserting a very strong secondary principle of liberty derived from utility but such that the good consequences of following the principle of liberty can be achieved only if we follow it without regard to the consequences, as an absolute principle. Whether this is a coherent position or not I will discuss later.

Mill says that the principle of liberty requires the most extensive liberty of speech and association and action compatible with not harming others. I shall not pursue the details of what he thinks it involves, as my concern at this point is with Mill's work as a theory of liberalism. So I take the liberal practices more or less for granted and consider why Mill thinks these practices best satisfy the principle of utility. A crucial part of Mill's account of the good consequences of the liberty principle involve his idea of the interests of "man" as a progressive being. These are best promoted first by allowing an extensive liberty of thought and expression. The great advantage of liberty in this sphere is that it is a condition of challenging error and of establishing truth. Even when a society already possesses true beliefs in some respect, liberty enables its members to acquire a better grasp of the reasons for holding them. Thus, let us say that the true beliefs of the society are that liberal practices are the best basis for social organization but that the theories available for understanding why we should adopt them are the unsatisfactory views of libertarian, utilitarian and the other theorists I discuss in Part III. Liberty will enable us to continue to evaluate the theories and produce better ones. However, these claims immediately raise the question of the utility of truth. Is truth a good in itself or only good for its consequences? Mill's answer is that the pursuit of truth for its own sake is an essential part of the interests of human beings as progressive beings. Only thus can we advance as a species by rejecting false beliefs and conceptions of the good and progressing to higher forms of life.

He uses a similar type of argument in favour of the value of individuality as an essential part of human well-being and necessary for the progress of the species to higher forms of life. Individuality is promoted by liberty because liberty allows individuals to choose for themselves what sort of life best suits them rather than have this determined for them by authority. But what is the good of individuality? In part it is instrumental. By leaving people free to choose how to live, liberty encourages innovation and originality and this brings about a dynamic and progressive society. In part individuality is a good in itself. It produces a great wealth and diversity of human beings who are "noble and beautiful objects of contemplation".[7]

MILL'S REFORM OF UTILITARIANISM

The above account of Mill's position includes two elements that look as though they cannot easily be accommodated in a utilitarian philosophy. The first is the idea of higher forms of life. Benthamite utilitarianism appears to be resolutely a matter of maximizing a quantity of net pleasure. Bentham says that pushpin is as good as poetry if the amount of pleasure is the same. Mill introduces a distinction between qualities of pleasure. Some pleasures are of higher nature than others. These are the pleasures of the mind as opposed to the pleasures of the body. They are qualitatively superior so they cannot be lumped together with lower pleasures in the calculation of a simple sum.[8] How Mill thinks we can arrive at a total is unclear, but to make the idea of higher pleasures itself compatible with utilitarianism we need the other element of Mill's reform noted above earlier. This is the idea that human beings can come to pursue certain ends for their own sake and at the same time and thereby make those ends part of the supreme end of happiness. He believes virtue can and should be pursued for its own sake. At first, we learn to do virtuous actions as means to our happiness but can come to treat it as an end in itself. Doing this will produce the best consequences. But we do it by finding our happiness in being virtuous and unhappiness in failing to achieve that standard. Thus, virtue for its own sake becomes incorporated in our idea of our happiness and an essential part of our end.[9] Individuality for its own sake can and should be treated similarly. In these ways, Mill includes ideal ends in the utility that is to be maximized and thereby the possibility of talking in terms of higher and lower forms of life.

Mill's strategy in these arguments has been to transform what look like principles that are valid independently of an appeal to the principle of utility, such as truth, virtue and individuality, into parts of the utilitarian end. Insofar as he does this the nature of the utilitarian end becomes more complex, but it remains a maximizing notion. There is a total of net utility to be promoted, although how to arrive at the composition of this total is not very clear. If maximizing a total remains the end, the standard criticisms of the maximizing principle remain also – namely, that it allows overriding of some people's fundamental interests for the sake of achieving a greater total. It does not entrench a distributive principle protecting such interests as a limit on maximization.

An alternative reading of Mill's strategy is to say that although the values of liberty, individuality, justice and so on are genuine secondary principles and are not to be incorporated in the end to be maximized, they are of such importance in human life that they have an absolute or near absolute status. This would mean that while they are so important because of their very good consequences, these consequences can only be achieved if we respect the requirements of liberty, justice and individuality without regard to the consequences. The trouble with this strategy is that a utilitarian fundamentally motivated by the duty to maximize cannot consistently pursue it, as I have pointed out earlier. He must always be aware that, as in the lawn-crossing example, even though the general practice of no lawn-crossings is in place, there will be a certain number of such lawn-crossings that, if permitted, would increase the total utility.

In other words, the absolute nature of the rule cannot be maintained. But if it is not maintained, the good effects of following the rule without regard to the consequences cannot be achieved.

To return to the absence of a limiting distributive principle in the standard formulation of the principle of utility, Mill is clearly aware of it and thinks he has overcome it by arguing that a distributive principle of equality is built into the very meaning of the idea of maximizing utility. His first shot at showing this claims that the principle of utility in telling us to maximize total net utility requires us to count each person's pleasure equally. He cites Bentham's supposed dictum to the effect that each person is to count for one and no one for more than one in the calculation of the total. He says that the principle has no rational signification unless it means that one person's happiness supposedly equal in degree (with due allowance made for kind) counts exactly as much as another's. In a footnote to this passage, Mill adds that in effect what the principle of utility tells us is that equal amounts of pleasure are equally desirable whether experienced by this or that person.[10]

Mill clearly thinks that these statements express a distributive principle of equality that is built into the principle of utility itself and thus that he has shown that it is not a simple instruction to maximize a total. But he is clearly wrong in supposing this. To maximize the total amount of pleasure over a number of people, one must indeed count equal amounts of pleasure as equally desirable whether they are experienced by this or that person. This is, however, simple maximization and says nothing about how the pleasures are to be distributed among people. In fact, Mill actually says that the principle of utility does not care who experiences these pleasures. So, from the perspective of that principle, a result that involved person A getting ten units of pleasure and person B getting minus two units, which produces a total surplus of eight units, would be better than a result in which both persons got three units of pleasure producing a total of only six units. Nevertheless, this confusion on Mill's part does not prevent him from continuing immediately to express his belief that what he has identified is an egalitarian distributive principle as part of the very meaning of the utility principle. For he expands on his remarks about equality thus: "the equal claim of everybody to happiness involves (in the estimation of the moralist and legislator) an equal claim to the means of happiness".[11] This statement expresses, indeed, a very strong egalitarian distributive principle which would severely limit the drive for maximization. The only trouble is that it does not follow from his previous statements about equality, and it does not follow from anything else that he has said. It stands only as an arbitrary assertion (because it is unjustified within the utilitarian philosophy) of individual right.

FURTHER READING

Bentham (1982), Parekh (1972) and Mill (2015).

On Bentham and Mill, read Hampsher-Monk (1992) and Boucher and Kelly (2003).

On utilitarianism in general, read Lyons (1965), Smart and Williams (1973) and Hare (1981).

NOTES

1 Bentham (1982, pp.159, 244).
2 Parekh (1972, p.196).
3 Bentham (1982, p.59).
4 Mill (2015, pp.12–13).
5 Ibid., p.13.
6 Ibid., p.14.
7 Ibid., p.62.
8 Ibid., pp.121–4.
9 Ibid., p.149.
10 Ibid., pp.174–5.
11 Ibid., p.175.

KANT'S IDEA OF FREEDOM AS RATIONAL SELF-DETERMINATION

INTRODUCTION

Kant (1724–1804) is probably the most influential ethical theorist of the modern era. Yet, he is little regarded as a political theorist (two recent large and impressive volumes on the major political thinkers don't even include a chapter on his work) and consequently as a liberal theorist. This is a mistake. His ethical theory can be actualized only through liberal forms of association. Thus, if he is of great importance as an ethical theorist and he elaborates that theory in political terms, so must he be as a liberal one.

The general idea of his ethics is that there exists a universal moral law which anyone who is a rational being can arrive at through submitting her natural desires to the demands of reason. As human beings are essentially rational beings, the moral law is not something external to and imposed on them, but rather a law derived from what is their own reason and thus one which they can and should impose on themselves. In determining themselves to will in accordance with the moral law, they are self-determining and so free from submission to an external will.

PRUDENTIAL RATIONALITY

How are human beings supposed to recognize and will this universal moral law as the law of their own being? We must begin with the individual learning to organize his own life through setting himself objectives or ends. Human beings in regard to their animal nature have impulses to action and, on the basis of such impulses, can choose to act in order to obtain the object they desire. Human beings have free choice. It arises in the choice of ends of action. This choice may be a normative act insofar as it establishes the end as a rule for the direction of one's future actions. Suppose that on seeing and hearing about the fate of Siberian tigers, I feel an impulse to save them. This may lead me to choose to give £100 to save the Siberian tigers. But the impulse may also lead me to adopt as a lasting objective of mine the saving of the Siberian tigers. That choice for Kant is a free normative choice because I am not determined to adopt it as a rule of action for myself by my impulses. I go beyond my impulses in choosing to determine my future actions by the rule that I set myself.[1]

In setting myself such an end, I commit myself to adopt appropriate means to the realization of the end. This commitment is an expression of reason in the control of my actions. It is not the original impulse that determines my choice of the end, neither does the original impulse compel me to adopt the appropriate means. However, it is certainly not another impulse that moves me to do the act that constitutes the means to the realization of the end. It is rather the universal character of reason that tells me that if I will the end, I must at the same time will whatever is the best appropriate means. It is a valid implication of whatever end I choose.

It follows for Kant that in organizing my life around the choice of ends for myself, I am forming my life in accordance with the dictates of reason. Furthermore, in choosing ends for her life, a person must have regard to the possible conflicts between these ends and to the fact that she is an enduring being and will have other ends in the future. Hence, she must seek to harmonize her ends from the perspective of her life as a whole. In doing this, Kant says that she has as her end her own happiness as a sum of satisfactions. He calls this her self-interest. The adoption of one's own happiness as one's overall end should be understood as a normative principle of prudential reason – in other words of reason as applied to one's own life as a separate and enduring entity rather than to the relations between human beings.

Kant believes that in imposing reason on one's actions in pursuit of one's ends, one is unifying one's life over time. Instead of being moved to act by a succession of impulses of the moment, one becomes conscious of oneself as one and the same will that is organizing a series of impulses so as to realize ends that this will has chosen. One acquires a self-consciousness as a free will that is at the same time a bestower of value on the things that it has chosen. In these respects a person is a being of special dignity, an end in itself and of absolute worth. That it has this character is because the self-imposition of reason is carried out unconditionally. It is not the result of some impulse or desire.

These claims do not seem particularly forceful to me, but I shall postpone a challenge to them for the moment. Although a rational agent is rationally required to make her own happiness her overall end, Kant does not believe that there are other universal requirements of prudential reason. This is because the ends people pursue under the concept of their happiness are so diverse that we cannot formulate necessary and universal rational requirements on the pursuit of happiness. At best, we can arrive at what Kant calls counsels of prudence.[2]

MORAL RATIONALITY

Prudential rationality is partially defective from the point of view of achieving full freedom through self-determination by reason. This is, in part, because one cannot derive necessary and universal rational requirements from the contingent content of people's happiness. But prudential reason is also deficient for Kant because the ends of action that are fundamental to prudential reason have a content that is overly determined by impulse. In order to choose to adopt as one's end the saving of the Siberian tiger, one must first have felt the impulse to save it and made this impulse into the basis of a rule of action. The impulse has been incorporated into the rule, and should it disappear and one no longer wants to save the Siberian tiger, following the rule loses its motivational point. One can't derive from pure reason the requirement to save the Siberian tiger. For full rational self-determination Kant wants something purer. This is his idea of morality as pure practical reason or pure reason determining human beings to action of itself.

To get to universal moral law from the notion of the semi-rational agent who has his own happiness as his end, we need the ideas of maxims of self-interest and the possibility of their universalization. Individual agents in accordance with their prudential reason will naturally aim at their own happiness and be inclined to formulate maxims of self-interest to guide their actions. They will think that it is alright for me to make a lying promise if it is in my interest to do so. At this point Kant believes that reason can assert itself in the form of a requirement to universalize one's maxim and turn it into a universal law for all rational beings. If one universalizes the lying maxim thus: everyone may make a lying promise when it is in their interest, the result will be that the practice of promising will disappear since no one will be able to trust another to keep his promises. The implication is that the maxim of lying promises is self-contradictory and must therefore be abandoned.[3]

There are two aspects to this argument: one is the requirement to universalize and the other is the claim to self-contradiction of universalizing the self-interested maxim. Why should one universalize one's maxim? Because reason does not permit you to say that it is OK for me to do X but not OK for you to do X, although there is no reason for this difference. Reason tells you that, if you are making a distinction, there must be a reason for it. The second aspect, however, fails. There is no self-contradiction in saying let everyone make lying promises and let the practice disappear. What the universalized maxim is incompatible with is your pursuit of your ends through making (lying) promises. You can benefit yourself from following the self-interested maxim only by free riding on the honesty of others who abide by the requirements of the practice. So you have got to will that others follow the practice but not yourself, and you cannot give a reason for making yourself an exception without its being valid for other selves also. In other words, you have to will universal egoism and non-cooperation through practices such as making promises.

The requirement to universalize expresses Kant's famous idea of a categorical imperative as the basis of morality. The categorical imperative is a requirement on our willing ends that is not conditional on our having particular desires for this or that substantive end. The requirement is unconditional and hence categorical whatever particular ends we have. Kant gives various formulations of this idea. The first formula is simply to will only what you can universalize. The fundamental idea here is, as we have seen in the example of lying promises, the exclusion of maxims of action that make oneself an exception to the universal law. However, as we saw also, this permits willing universal egoism. Hence, to get to something moral and beneficial for human beings you have to suppose that they desire to pursue their own ends through cooperation with others according to common laws. But that move destroys the unconditional and categorical nature of the cooperative laws. Kant's next formulation of the categorical imperative does no better. It is the idea of willing your maxims as though they were universal laws of nature i.e. that everyone actually behaves in accordance with the rational requirements. Since this also does not exclude universal non-cooperative egoism – for purely egoistic interaction is a possible world, although cooperators would do much better – it fails for the same reason.

The third formulation introduces a new and very influential idea. The formula is that in our willing we should always treat humanity (human beings) as an end in itself and never as a means only. Human beings are ends in themselves by virtue of being rational beings. So the formula presupposes that rational being is an end in itself. A being that is an end in itself is a being of absolute worth. Absolute worth is contrasted with relative worth. Something of relative worth has its worth dependent on something else which, if that other thing ceases to be, removes the worth of the original entity. Kant supposes that absolute worth asserts itself in human beings through the self-imposition of rational requirements on willing. When a human being imposes rational requirements on the pursuit of his own ends – he must adopt the best means to achieve his ends; he must harmonize his ends with each other and over time as the elements of a whole that is his happiness – he necessarily represents his rational will to himself as an end in itself. The self-imposition of reason on his pursuit of his particular ends is not conditional on his choice of ends. It is an end in itself. I take this to mean that reason's asserting itself in a person's will is done unconditionally i.e. not because he desires some other end which reason helps him to achieve.[4]

Since each human being in actualizing reason in his life must represent himself to himself in the same way as an end in himself and a being of absolute worth, the formula of humanity necessarily follows. Each rational being must treat all the others as ends in themselves for him, as beings of absolute worth, and never as means only. This formula clearly does away with the problem of universal egoism, but it has its own problems. Why should rational will that asserts itself in a particular person treat that person as a unity over time and seek to organize that person's ends as a single whole? Rational will has in itself no more interest in the ends of that person than in the ends of any other person. It is because the person becomes conscious of himself as a unity over time that it makes sense for him to use his reason in constructing a conception of his good as a whole over time. Kant has got the argument the wrong way round. Kant thinks that reason imposes the unity on his life by organizing his ends over time as the ends of a single person and that without reason this unification would not take place. Reversing Kant's argument, however, undermines the idea of rational being as an end in itself, a being of absolute worth. For, if reason's construction of a person's good over time depends on that person's prior self-understanding as an enduring being and hence on his having the idea of that being's good over his life, then reason will not be unconditional but dependent on his desire for his good as he conceives this as something to be actualized over time.

If we accept that criticism of the formula of humanity, it not only undermines the unconditional nature of reason but also makes possible again the willing of universal egoism. For, the rational organization of a single person's life as a whole now cannot represent itself to that person as the willing of a being that is an end in itself. It can only represent itself to itself as an end FOR itself. Universalizing that brings us back to universal egoism. Kant has one final reformulation of the categorical imperative: this is the formula of the realm of ends and autonomy of the will. With regard to the realm of ends, the formula require us to act in accordance with the maxims of a universally legislative member of a possible realm of ends. A realm is a systematic union of different rational beings through common laws, and a realm of ends is one in which the ends of the union of rational beings must be mutually supportive. The idea of the autonomy of the will is just the idea of the rational will as a self-legislative will that has no other end than its own self-determination.

The rational will as a being of absolute worth having itself as its own end is the ground of the whole system of morality.[5]

This is heady stuff and it becomes headier still in subsequent German philosophers such as Fichte and Hegel whose ideas I shall not attempt to describe. The final Kantian formula appealing to a community of rational beings clearly does not follow from the idea of a universalizing reason if you accept my reasoning in these paragraphs. There is no way we can sustain a conception of reason as an unconditional, self-legislating eruption in human beings' lives. We have to think of it, in its practical form, as driven by our desires to pursue our own good over time and through cooperation with others under common practices. Reason develops the forms through which these non-rational ends can best be achieved.

KANT'S LIBERALISM

The structure of Kant's ethics has strong liberal implications. In order for a human being to develop fully his potential for rational willing, he must go through a process of organizing his particular ends in accordance with reason in the manner described earlier. He must choose the best means to realize his ends and must unify his life over time by making his life as a whole his end. Since the construction of this end is done by reason and has no other point but its own existence, it must be conceived as an end in itself. This, then, is how each person in organizing his life in accordance with reason must conceive himself. As a rational being in his particular life, he is an end in himself. This is only a stage on the way to his understanding that every other human being as a rational being represents his particular life to himself in the same way and thus that all such beings are ends in themselves. In grasping the formula of humanity, the individual realizes that he has to impose on his pursuit of his particular good a universal will that all other rational beings could will also from their perspective.

This process requires liberal forms, because in order to rationally order one's life, one must be in charge of it. One must be able to do things in the external world that are the result of one's willing particular ends of one's own choosing. In particular, one must have command of some external resources or private property to be able to decide on and carry out a course of action in the world aimed at the achievement of such self-chosen ends. One needs what Kant calls external freedom. This structure of ethical development, thus, requires a sphere of negative freedom so that the autonomy of the will can actualize itself as the self-imposition of reason. The sphere of negative freedom is the necessary liberal content of Kantian ethics.

KANT'S THEORY OF THE STATE

The sphere of negative freedom consists of those actions that are not forbidden by the system of universal legislation. This is the area of my lawful freedom.

My freedom in this area is consistent with the freedom of everyone else under universal law.[6] Insofar as I am exercising and defending my freedom, I am acting in accordance with my rational will, but I am not necessarily imposing my rational will on my actions. I could be acting in accordance with universal law because others are threatening me with consequences if I seek to invade their freedom. So, I may be keeping within the law not from a moral motive but from a prudential one. Nevertheless, I would be acting justly, in Kant's view. Justice is "the possibility of the conjunction of universal reciprocal coercion with the freedom of everyone in accordance with universal laws".[7] The sphere of coercion is for Kant the appropriate sphere for state action. The state is the institution that can best take over the activity of coercing everyone to remain within the limits of their lawful freedom.

Without the state we would exist in a state of nature in which our rights to our lawful freedom would be very insecure and indeterminate. The main sphere of this insecurity consists in our property rights. We must be able to appropriate parts of the earth's surface as the location of our external freedom, and we can acquire such rights through appropriating what is not already the property of another. But I am only bound to respect the rights of others in accordance with universal law if the law is actualized in the will of others through their respect for my rights. In a state of nature, there can be no guarantee that such reciprocal respect will be observed. No individual can provide such a guarantee with regard to the enforcement of property rights, since the will of an individual in such matters would be an arbitrary imposition of his will on all the others and hence unacceptable to them. What is required is a will binding on everyone and that is "a collective, universal (common) and powerful will". Such a will is to be found in a properly constituted state.[8] Kant concludes that everyone is entitled to compel others with whom he comes into conflict over property rights to enter with him into a political union.[9]

A properly constituted state is a union of a multitude of people under laws of justice, as defined earlier. The supreme authority in the state is the legislative body which can only be attributed to the united will of the people. He sees this will as incapable of doing injustice to the people, because no one can be said to do an injustice to himself when he is the decider. Since the supreme legislative will is the united will of the people, each decides the same for all and all decide the same for each. The executive and judicial branches of government are subordinate to and instruments of this general will of the people. The ethical justification for the state in Kant's theory is that it alone can create the conditions under which a universal rational will can be actualized. What ethically speaking I should do is to impose a universal rational will on my particular choices and actions. But under the most complete formulation of the categorical imperative, I am required to will as a universally legislative member of a realm of ends, and that involves a union in which the ends of the members are mutually supportive. However, while I can formulate the idea of such a universal rational will, there is no way I can actually impose such a will on my choices and actions in the real world without being a member of an actual community that aims at the harmony of its members' ends. So, something like the state is the necessary vehicle of the ethical will. The state itself is not an ethical will insofar as it is not the free self-imposition of rational will but is an expression of universal reciprocal coercion consistent with the freedom of all. Yet, it creates the very same forms that the ethical will needs for its own actualization.

THE STATUS OF THE INDIVIDUAL IN KANT'S ETHICS

I have already given reasons for rejecting Kant's inflated conception of reason. His theory also has serious implications for the ethical status of individuals. On the face of it, his theory appears to attach extraordinary weight to the individual's value. The individual is an end in himself and a being of absolute worth. But we have to ask: in respect of what feature of the individual human being is he of absolute worth? The answer is quite clear. It is not in virtue of his particular existence as Joe Blogs or Paul Smith that an individual has this extraordinary status. If it were, then Joe Blogs' particular interests and ends would have that absolute worth and that would be an impossible world. It is in virtue of Joe Blogs' particular existence being the way in which a universal rational will can actualize itself. Of course, Joe Blogs has to make this will his will by imposing it on his choices and actions. But what is of absolute worth is the universal rational will which becomes Joe Blogs' actual will. Insofar as Joe fails to will the universal, he is not of absolute worth. He is at best a potential vehicle for it. The implication is that whether Joe Blogs or Paul Smith, as particular beings, exist or not is not all that important from the point of view of the self-actualization of universal rational will. Particular vehicles are needed but not this or that person or even this or that state. This does not seem to me an attractive or credible view of the ethical status of individual human beings (or that of states for that matter).

FURTHER READING

Kant (1965, 1993).
On Kant's ethics, read Hill (1992), Wood (1999); on his political philosophy, read Flikschuh (2000).

NOTES

1 Kant (1993, pp.25–8).
2 Ibid., pp.27–8.
3 Ibid., pp.14–15.
4 Ibid., pp.35–6.
5 Ibid., p.43.
6 Kant (1965, p.35).
7 Ibid., pp.36–7.
8 Ibid., pp.77–8.
9 Ibid., p.71.

CONTEMPORARY THEORIES OF LIBERALISM

THE THEORY OF JOHN RAWLS (1921–2002): LIBERALISM AS NEUTRAL BETWEEN DIFFERENT CONCEPTIONS OF THE GOOD

The first half of the 20th century saw a remarkable decline in philosophical thinking about ethics and politics in the western world. Instead of philosophical debate about ethical and political values, the intellectual world was filled with ideological claims that were widely seen as lacking a rational basis. In the academies, doubts were expressed as to whether the subjects still existed. In this context the development and publication of Rawls's theory of justice came to be seen as the moment when new life was breathed into these traditional forms. It is certainly the case that since then, there has been a massive increase in the amount of academic work in these fields.

I shall concentrate on Rawls's first book *A Theory of Justice* (rev. ed. 1999). It was this book that created the new interest in, and fuelled the new hope for, political philosophy as a rational enterprise. His second book *Political Liberalism* (1993) seemed to be a betrayal of that promise. *A Theory of Justice* was avowedly a liberal theory and became so influential that liberalism itself has come to be identified by many with the new paradigm established by that book. This is a serious mistake.

What is distinctive about Rawls's approach to political values and the defence of liberalism from a historical perspective is his claim that liberalism is neutral between different conceptions of the good. This appears to be a bizarre way of defending liberal values. If there are specific values that a liberal way of life is committed to – such as freedom and equality – then, presumably, in order to defend these, you have to show that they are superior values to the alternatives on offer or that they are rationally required and so have no acceptable alternatives. From the beginning, Rawls was criticized by some for not in fact sticking to his programme but disguising the dependence of his theory on the standard liberal values through a complex obfuscatory framework. With this in mind, let us see how his theory is supposed to work.

Rawls supposes that the members of an existing political society, reflecting on the adequacy from an ethical point of view of their present laws and institutions, decide to commit themselves to those principles that they could all agree on in a new contract.[1] However, they are to approach this debate from behind a veil of ignorance.

A veil of ignorance obscures from each person all knowledge of her particular attributes – her sex, age, abilities, preferences, conception of the good, and her social and economic position; in short, her natural and social assets. The veil leaves her with only general knowledge of human beings and human society.[2] Rawls believes that the veil requires each person to choose as though she had an equal chance of being anyone.

What the contractors are supposed to know about human beings in general is that there are certain primary social goods which are good for all human beings. These are liberty, opportunity, income, wealth and the bases of self-respect.[3] They are social, because they are produced through modes of social interaction. They are primary, because they are good for human beings to have whatever their particular characteristics and conceptions of the good. They will do better if they have more of these goods rather than less. At least no one will be harmed by having more than he needs. In a subsequent publication – *The Dewey Lectures* – Rawls identified two other features of human beings that were implicit in his account.[4] They have two fundamental moral powers and corresponding to them two higher order interests. These are, first, the capacity to form their lives around a conception of the good and, second, a sense of justice.

What they know about society is that it is a cooperative arrangement for mutual advantage. All can be better off cooperating under common norms than as independents. The problem facing the contractors is, then, what norms governing the distribution of the social primary goods can they all agree on?

Rawls calls his theory justice as fairness. This is because the procedure he adopts for determining valid norms is presented as a fair one. Nobody is advantaged or disadvantaged by this procedure, because without particular knowledge of one's interests one cannot attempt to secure a result that benefits oneself or those like oneself at the expense of the rest. Without that particular knowledge, all that a person can hope for, for herself, is as much of the primary social goods as possible. However, since there is no way in which she could secure more for herself than others, she will go for an initial equal distribution of these goods: an equal liberty, equal opportunity, equal income and wealth, and the bases of self-respect. Insofar as this result is an identifiably liberal one, albeit of an extreme egalitarian kind, then Rawls appears to have found a way of justifying liberalism without grounding it in specifically liberal values. His liberalism appears to be neutral between different conceptions of the good.

Rawls claims that in the original contractual situation people would choose a modification of the initial equal distribution of the primary social goods, which he calls the difference principle. This principle says that an unequal distribution that is to the greatest benefit of the least advantaged group in society is just. This modification applies only to the distribution of income and wealth and not to the distribution of liberties and opportunities. So, the developed conception of justice as fairness yields two principles – the equal liberties principle and the difference principle which requires at the same time that opportunities to achieve positions of wealth and power should meet a standard of fair equality.[5]

Rawls's contractors are supposedly faced with a choice between a number of possible normative systems. These are: justice as fairness, utilitarianism, mixed conceptions, perfectionism and intuitionism.[6] Rawls consistently treats utilitarianism as the main challenger to justice as fairness. His main objection to utilitarianism is that it allows losses to some people to be overridden by greater gains accruing to others. People in the contractual situation would not choose such a scheme, because behind the veil of ignorance they would not know whether they might not turn out to be one of those suffering for the greater good. Perfectionism comprises all those conceptions of justice in which the social order is organized from the point of view of the achievement of excellence according to some standard of the good. Examples of perfectionist doctrines are Platonism and theological conceptions of how human beings should live. These doctrines define the end that all humans should have. They reject an equal liberty for adherents of different views of the good and privilege both the preferred doctrine and the persons who have superior knowledge of it. However, the contractors would reject perfectionist systems because they do not know what their conception of the good is or indeed whether they are perfectionists rather than pluralists in respect of the good life for human beings. To vote for an indeterminate perfectionist system would be senseless, and to vote for any particular one without knowing that it was what you believed was the truth about the good would be equally senseless.

By intuitionism Rawls means schemes under which a variety of conflicting principles are balanced against each other in particular situations with a view to reaching a judgement based on intuition as to what is just in that case. The inconveniences and indeterminacy of such a procedure are obvious. That leaves the contractors with mixed conceptions and justice as fairness. An example of a mixed conception would be utility-maximizing subject to a constraint requiring a minimum level of social primary goods for all. Rawls does discuss such possibilities but rejects them, since justice as fairness offers a better deal to the potentially worst off group.

The reasoning behind the choice of the difference principle is that it would be irrational for the contractors to prefer the initial absolute equality over the difference principle, because under the latter everyone would enjoy a higher level of the primary social goods, including the worst off group. Indeed, the difference principle ensures that this group will be in a better position than under any alternative scheme.

It may look surprising that Rawls does not offer his contractors the opportunity to adopt a version of the libertarian principle. In fact, he treats it as a possible principle for determining the distribution of income and wealth under the name of the system of natural liberty. The obvious reason for his not offering libertarianism as a full system of justice in competition with the others is that it fully accepts Rawls's first principle of justice – namely the equal liberties principle – and only differs from justice as fairness in respect of the second principle. The system of natural liberty is rejected as a competitor to the difference and opportunities principle on the grounds that it allows people to be advantaged and disadvantaged on the basis of their unequal natural and social assets. Rawls believes this is profoundly unjust since no one deserves their position in this natural lottery.

There exists a voluminous literature on the details of the two principles, but I shall ignore this and concentrate on whether Rawls's theory of justice is actually a theory of liberalism as I have been understanding the requirements for such a theory. On the face of it, it purports to show why the members of a political society should choose liberal forms of political association with a fairly strong egalitarian tendency. But this may be doubted. We have to ask why the members should agree to debate the problem of what norms should govern their association from behind a veil of ignorance. Suppose that their polity is at present organized on the basis of the truth of Sunni Islam. While adherents of this faith are in a majority, there are other non-Islamic and non-Sunni groups in the society. Why would the majority think that the veil of ignorance condition is fair? From their point of view, they possess the truth about the good, and other groups with inferior understanding may be allowed some degree of freedom to practise their faith and run their lives. But they cannot be treated as equal citizens of their polity enjoying equal liberties and opportunities. In other words, they would not accept the veil of ignorance as fair.

In fact, a necessary condition for the veil to appear reasonable would be that the members were pluralists about the good. They believe that there are many different conceptions of the human good, and what is important to them is their right to determine for themselves what to believe and how to live. In those circumstances, they would think it unreasonable for the adherents of any particular conception of the good to impose their beliefs on the whole society, and so they would have no objection in this regard to the veil. But in that case the anti-perfectionist result of the operation of the veil would merely express the anti-perfectionism which the members already accepted. It could not justify it. This is more or less what Rawls is committing himself to in his conception of the human beings' higher order interest in forming and living by a particular conception of the good. I say more or less, because strictly speaking this higher order interest is compatible with the belief that there is an objectively valid understanding of the human good, and their higher order interest lies in perfecting themselves in relation to it. Behind a veil of ignorance, they do not know what it is. But included in their general knowledge of the human condition generally could be the knowledge that there is such a good. In that case the contractors would choose an arrangement which gave special attention to the development of knowledge of the good, for instance by giving preferential treatment to philosophers! We see, then, that a condition for the acceptance of the veil is the belief in pluralism about the good. Given the belief in pluralism, the higher order interest of humans in developing and living by their particular conception of the good will in fact be an expression of the liberal valuation of human beings' capacity for autonomy.

The veil ensures that the members are situated in relation to each other as equals in worth and power. Behind the veil, there is no way in which anyone can gain an advantage over the others. Nevertheless, could they not think that a fair distributive principle would be to each according to her contributions or according to her desert? Would the better endowed, at least, not object to the veil on these grounds? However, the members are not supposed to have any intuitions about justice at this point. Justice is supposed to be the result of the agreement behind the veil, and that agreement is supposed to be reached as a result of everyone trying to maximize her supply of social primary goods under conditions in which no one can propose rules advantageous to herself since no one knows what would give her a relative advantage. Their sense of justice is the capacity that once what is just is identified through the contract, enables them to abide by the contract's terms. From that point of view, the superior natural assets of the better endowed constitute an advantage that is not deserved and should be discounted. So knowledge of it is put behind the veil. But once again this function of the veil expresses the conception of human beings as of equal worth regardless of natural inequalities and hence entitled to an equal power. It does not justify that conception.

Effectively, then, no one would accept Rawls's agreement situation — the veil plus the supposed general interests of human beings — who was not already committed to egalitarian liberal presuppositions. These are, in Rawls's case, the conception of persons as having a fundamental interest in forming and pursuing conceptions of the good under conditions of pluralism about values, on the one hand, and as being of equal worth regardless of natural inequalities, on the other, and hence entitled to an equal power. In other words, the "theory" presupposes that the contractors are conceived, and conceive themselves, to be free and equal persons. Consequently, Rawls's theory cannot be represented as a justificatory theory of liberalism, despite the original belief that that was what he was doing and had achieved, because it takes for granted what a theory is supposed to establish. Thus, it is not a new type of justificatory liberal theory based on the idea of liberalism as being neutral between different conceptions of the good. The only neutrality involved is between conceptions of the good held by liberals in liberal forms. There is no neutrality between liberal values and anti-liberal values. One might say, how could there be? In that case, Rawls's answer to the question, why should we be liberals? is, in effect, we already are. But that, since there is no necessity to our being liberals, is no answer at all.

Rawls might be taken to be answering the different question: what sort of liberal should we be? He looks to be, and certainly sees himself as, a fairly radical egalitarian. But how radical he is depends on the implications for the distribution of income and wealth of the difference principle. For instance, the tax changes that the Trump administration has recently introduced in the United States give massive gains to the very rich and smaller and smaller gains to people as they are lower down on the income scale, with the result that the worst-off group gets a miserly few dollars a year extra. The Republicans can, in fact, justify the grossly disproportionate gains to the rich in Rawlsian terms if it is the case that the minuscule improvement in the position of the worst off is the result of the changes to the position of the rich. Rawls himself believes that as a society gets wealthier, the application of the difference principle will produce a more egalitarian society. However, this is an empirical matter and his belief can certainly be disputed.

The initial egalitarianism that Rawls endorses is, as we have seen, presupposed by his adoption of the veil of ignorance and follows from his belief that a social order is unjust if it allows people to become better or worse off than others because of their place in the natural lottery that is the distribution of genetic assets. This idea is fundamental to liberal egalitarianism. It is developed by Ronald Dworkin in a distinctive form that I will discuss in the next section.

Rawls produced another major work entitled *Political Liberalism* several years later in which he reformulates the ideas of *A Theory of Justice* in response to the intense scrutiny that had been given to the first work. In the later work Rawls presents his theory as a political not metaphysical or comprehensive account of liberalism. By a metaphysical or comprehensive account, Rawls means one that is dependent for its validity on the truth of a comprehensive or substantive ethical theory such as utilitarianism or Kantianism or libertarianism. The trouble with such dependency is that the theories are disputable. The truth on these matters cannot be established beyond reasonable doubt. But if the case for liberalism rests on such grounds, then some people will reasonably reject these grounds, and then a liberal regime will have no legitimacy for them. A theory of liberalism that is political will be one that is justifiable to everyone whatever comprehensive theory of the good they hold.

Despite the standard treatment of *Political Liberalism* as involving a shift in Rawls's thought towards the political, it is not clear to me that this is the correct view. It is true that substantive ethical commitments to the liberal values of freedom and equality are present in *A Theory of Justice*. But they are concealed within the framework of the original position and the veil of ignorance. The official doctrine of the book is that the theory is neutral between different conceptions of the good. On this view *Political Liberalism* involves another shot at justifying liberalism independently of any substantive ethical theory.

He thinks that this can be done by elaborating the liberal conception of society "in terms of fundamental ideas viewed as implicit in the public-political culture of a democratic society".[7] This assumes that the liberal ideas are embedded in our actual institutions and practices and hence are implicitly shared by all. *Political Liberalism*, by making these ideas explicit, reveals a consensus among citizens on the legitimacy of the practices despite the fact that they believe in their legitimacy on the basis of different conceptions of the good. Some will be utilitarians, others natural rights thinkers and yet others, Kantians. Rawls calls this an overlapping consensus.

From my point of view – namely that of a theory of liberalism – this programme will not yield a theory at all. In effect, one way of carrying out this programme would be to do what I have been doing in the first two Parts of this book. You begin with an account of the practices of a liberal society, as I have done in Part I. You then proceed to elicit from these practices an account of the values embedded in them. This shows that insofar as the citizens of this liberal society accept and follow the practices, they are committed to the liberal values embedded in them as their values. Hence, everyone, or at least the great majority, accepts the legitimacy of liberalism.

The trouble with this programme is not only that it omits the whole dimension of real theorizing about these practices contained in my Part III. It also leaves unresolved the conflict at the practical level between disputed understandings of the liberal values. The different implications of these understandings for how the practice should actually be carried on are brushed away for the sake of emphasizing the fact of agreement on the essentials that constitute the overlapping consensus. From this perspective Rawls has to accept that his account of liberalism in *A Theory of Justice* in terms of justice as fairness is just one view among others in the overlapping consensus.

My main objection to the programme of *Political Liberalism*, however, remains the fact that it is not a real theory of the kind needed to justify liberalism. The idea of grounding the legitimacy of liberalism in an overlapping consensus does so only from a subjective point of view. A regime may be said to be legitimate for its citizens if the great majority endorse the values embedded in its institutions and practices. But this is merely to say that they believe their regime to be justifiable from an objective point of view. This belief may be entirely mistaken. This possibility Rawls does not discuss. In effect, Rawls does not believe that objective theorizing about liberalism and its competitors is possible at all.

THE "COMPREHENSIVE" LIBERALISM OF RONALD DWORKIN (1931–2013)

Rawls's conception of human beings is that they have the capacity for autonomy – the moral power of forming and living by conceptions of the good – and that they see each other as equals. Human beings as free and equal are the foundations of a liberal society. But why we should attach a value to the capacity for autonomy or see each other as equals, he does not know, since his whole theory is based on his not being able to tell us. Ronald Dworkin has no such inhibitions. Dworkin was an important philosopher of law as well as of politics and was Professor of Jurisprudence at Oxford University as well as Professor of Law and Philosophy at New York University. His account of the two features of human life – autonomy and equality – is broadly Kantian in character. It is, thus, certainly a justificatory theory of liberalism but one that has the defects of the Kantian approach. Although Dworkin's account of liberalism is grounded in a comprehensive conception of the good, he believes this account is anti-perfectionist in nature.

Dworkin maintains that of the two principles – freedom and equality – it is equality that must be given precedence and freedom interpreted in its light. His foundational principle of equality he formulates as the requirement to treat people with equal concern and respect.[8] This obviously prompts the question why we should treat people in this way and what is it to show concern and respect. His answer becomes more elaborate over his many works but let us begin with the earliest and simplest formulations. Thus, in his *Taking Rights Seriously* (1977), his answer is that we are required to show such concern because human beings have the capacity to make plans and give justice. To show concern and respect for these reasons, then, would involve, it would seem, being concerned that human beings had the opportunities and liberties to develop and give effect to this capacity and similarly with their sense of justice. Later he describes the ideal of equality as the view that life matters and matters equally. One obvious weakness in these claims is that it is highly likely that people possess the capacity to make plans to different degrees. So if worth depends on capacity and this is possessed unequally, it should follow that people will be of unequal worth and, hence, concern and respect should be unequal. Also, if lives matter, why does it follow that lives matter equally? Some people live more valuable lives than others. They are bearers of truth or goodness while others lead despicable or evil lives.

This problem appears to arise because the source of worth is treated as an empirical attribute of people and thus can be possessed to different degrees – such as the ability to make plans for one's life. Perhaps all that is needed is the idea of a threshold level of the capacity that everyone can achieve and that once achieved brings the worth inherent in the attribute into being. It would not be the degree to which one possesses the attribute that creates the worth but the mere possession of the capacity beyond the threshold level. Everyone beyond the threshold can be said to possess the capacity while abstracting from the inequalities in the degree of its possession. Nevertheless, it is difficult to see why, in identifying worth, one should disregard the inequalities unless what the threshold level brings into being is some ethical entity, like Kant's self-determining rational will, that supervenes immediately upon the attainment of the threshold.

Dworkin invokes the idea of intrinsic importance that attaches to lives in a passage in which he responds to a challenge from Jan Narveson to justify his egalitarianism.[9] His argument is the following: each person thinks that it is important how his life goes. That it is important how his life goes presupposes that his life has intrinsic importance. If his life is of intrinsic importance because it is important how his life goes, then exactly the same reasoning applies to every other person. Hence, the lives of all persons are of equal intrinsic importance.

This argument is certainly invalid. Each person may, in making decisions for his life, treat how his life goes as of importance for himself, and we may conclude that therefore he treats his life as an end of intrinsic importance. But this shows only that his life is of intrinsic importance for himself. The idea that it is of intrinsic importance in itself or for everyone is completely unwarranted.

The idea of intrinsic importance is the idea of something being of value in itself or as an end of action rather than of instrumental value as a means to the achievement of some other end. This would seem to be similar to Kant's view of the person as an end in herself.

On Kant's view, each person in organizing her life as a whole over time treats it as an end in itself. Since everyone does this, all persons must be treated as equally ends in themselves and never as means only. However, for Kant, the quality of being an end is an attribute of rational will that is only partially realized in the particular individual and more fully realized in the universal ethical will comprehending all rational persons. The particular individual then realized his inherent worth only insofar as the content of his willing was governed by the demands of the universal ethical will. Dworkin, and innumerable others, treat intrinsic importance as an attribute of the particular individual. Each individual is of intrinsic importance. But it is supposed to follow from this that all are of equal importance in such a way that the requirement to respect universal equality takes precedence over the validity of any plans one makes for one's life. The only plans that are acceptable are those that are compatible with the demands of equality. Since each person treats his life as of intrinsic importance in itself and so independently of his relation to others, he has no reason to subordinate his will to the demands of equality as the theory requires. For these reasons, Dworkin's theory of liberalism cannot be considered to be successful.

Much of Dowrkin's influence on liberal thought, however, has not been through his gestures towards a justificatory theory, the form of which he shares with many others, but through his work on how best to understand the requirements of equality.[10] This theory of equality is an important modification of the egalitarian interpretation of liberalism developed by Rawls. So, I shall sketch it in and add some critical comments. Dworkin, first of all, rejects accounts of how to achieve equality that involve some administrator distributing what she takes to be an equality of welfare to all individuals. Quite apart from the arbitrary power this scheme would give to the administrator, it would not pay attention to the importance in a person's well-being of her own conception of how she wants her life to go – in other words, her choice of ends. But if the administrator seeks information from each person about their plans for their lives and then tries to ensure that each is provided with the resources enabling her to attain the same level of well-being from her efforts to carry out her plans as everyone else attains from their efforts, everybody would have a strong incentive to exaggerate her initial claims so as to increase her share of resources. The ambitions of the scheme – the idea of an administrator distributing resources so as to equalize people's level of well-being – are, no doubt, deluded also. But Dworkin's point is certainly valid that we need to ensure that there is first of all a fair distribution of resources before asking people to make their plans for their lives rather than the other way round. They must choose their plans in the light of the resources they are entitled to.

Dworkin's aim is, then, to achieve an initial distribution of resources that can be said to be equal while taking account of the fact that a person's choice of her ends may have effects on the availability of resources to others and hence may impose costs on them. He models such a distribution in the following way: a collection of people are stranded on an uninhabited island that contains a sufficiency but not an abundance of resources. In order to achieve a fair distribution of the resources among themselves, each is given the same quantity of counters and invited to make bids for the resources she thinks she would need for the life she wants to lead. What she can get with her counters depends on how much of what she wants exists and how many other bids for the same resources there are. If, at the end of a round of bidding, some people are dissatisfied with their outcome, the bidding may be restarted until everyone is satisfied that in the circumstances of the existing supply and demand for resources, she has got the best deal she could expect.

The point of this model for Dworkin is that it seeks to combine the aspiration to a substantive equality with respect for the autonomy of persons in the choice of plans for their lives. Such autonomy can be enjoyed only if it is protected by liberty rights entitling people to make and execute their personal choices. But liberty of this kind is highly likely to result in an unequal distribution of resources. Some people will be more effective planners and traders then others because of their natural abilities; some will do better because of luck in their initial choice of resources; yet others may have decided to work hard and accumulate resources while fellow islanders enjoyed a costless leisure on their island's abundant beaches. Dworkin's view is that some of these inequalities may be justified but not others. If autonomy is to be protected, then people must be allowed to make choices and benefit from them provided that the outcome can be attributed to a free choice which anyone could have made had they decided to do so. If people made different, but free, choices as a result of which they are worse off in terms of resources than me, then the inequality is justified. But if the outcome is in whole or in part attributable to my luck in being born smarter than you or due to other circumstance for which I am not responsible – such as illness or natural disasters – then the resulting inequality is not justified. This conception of egalitarianism has come to be called luck egalitarianism. The basic idea is that no one should be better or worse off than another through circumstances for which she is not responsible, and among such circumstances are a person's natural abilities. Dworkin thinks that his market model of equal distribution can accommodate the luck egalitarian principle by including an insurance scheme in which people insure themselves behind a veil of ignorance against turning out to be disadvantaged. Under this scheme the compensation given to those who turned out to be disadvantaged is paid for out of the premiums that the advantaged paid in without any return.

The idea of luck egalitarianism is a modification of Rawls's scheme of justice. The veil of ignorance in Rawls's scheme serves to insure that no one can gain from his superior natural abilities without having to compensate the worse off through the operation of the difference principle. But it also requires those who become better off as a result of their life choices rather than their natural abilities to compensate those who become worse off through their life choices. This is unfair according to Dworkin and his fellow luck egalitarians. Furthermore, Rawls's principles in applying only to those who are cooperators for mutual advantage do not make allowance for the disabled. On both these counts luck egalitarianism claims to be a superior version of a qualified egalitarianism.

Luck egalitarianism has been roundly criticized for its counter-intuitive consequences. A person who becomes destitute through his own free but bad choices is not entitled to any welfare, while the person who freely chose to gamble her resources and made a killing is entitled to retain all her gains. Furthermore, luck egalitarian officials involved in compensating people for their natural inferiority would thereby be demeaning the very people they were trying to help as well as having to intrude on people's lives to establish whether or not their condition was due to circumstances for which they were not responsible.

However, the very idea of counting a person's natural abilities as belonging to her circumstances rather than to her very own self as a unity of will and body is surely mistaken. A person's autonomy only makes sense as a developed natural ability to develop her other natural abilities in accordance with her choices. Thus, if a person develops the ambition of developing her natural musical abilities in order to become a professional pianist, she must see her natural musical abilities as an integral part of who she is and of what she wants to become – not as part of her circumstances. All these together make a self such that no part can be considered as external to herself. Of course, if she loses her fingers in some unfortunate accident, her self must re-order itself and its plans in accordance with its reduced abilities. That the luck egalitarian position has any plausibility is because of the basis of this doctrine in a metaphysical conception of a person as a being of intrinsic importance or absolute worth in virtue of being essentially a free will. However, we should not think of a free will as an independent substance only contingently connected to a body, but as necessarily embedded in and operative through a body and its capacities that it has to identify itself with as its very own in order to be able to move them to action in the first place. If a person's capacities are an integral part of being a self, they cannot at the same time be seen as part of her circumstances.

One of the problems in Dowrkin's theory of liberalism is his account of the state. For Rawls, the existence of independent political societies is presupposed in his theory. His contractors are members of such a society attempting to evaluate their existing practices. They are legislating for themselves and not for humanity. But Dowrkin's theory is a universalist ethic in form since the claim to the intrinsic importance of one's life applies to all human lives, as does the claim that all such lives are equally important. So one would think that the status of an independent political society in such a scheme would be that of constituting a way station on the road to a world state in which the equality of everyone could be directly achieved. But actually from his earliest theorizing, he has treated the ethic of equal concern and respect as constituting a political morality only, as applying only to the members of a state to govern their relations and not the relations of everybody in the world.[11] In fact, in his latest book, he allows that the doctrine of the intrinsic importance of human lives translates into a universal ethic of limited character – a universal humanitarian law. The full doctrine of equal concern and respect still only applies to relations between citizens of a state. His only explanation of this restriction of scope is that relations between citizens are conducted through a separate artificial and collective entity that is the state, and in such an institution the full requirements of equal concern and respect are mandated. He seems to be saying that full socio-economic justice applies because the state is a collective entity in which the citizens are responsible for making the rules as well as for submitting to them.[12] This may describe a feature of the state but hardly justifies the claim being made about the restricted scope of socio-economic justice. It is only if that feature of the state identifies it as a community through which the ethical claims of persons on each other arise in the first place that Dworkin's claim would hold. If, as he believes, the underlying ethical values are inherently of universal scope, their restriction of scope to separate states is acceptable only as a moment in the progress to a universal ethical community.

I said earlier that Dworkin claims to be an anti-perfectionist despite grounding his theory in a comprehensive theory of the good of Kantian inspiration. In this respect he follows Nozick's view of his own autonomy-based theory of liberalism as anti- perfectionist in character. What they understand by anti-perfectionism is that the state should not be in the business of promoting any substantive ideal of the good life. This is clearly a deluded view of the character of their own theories, since for the state to promote an autonomous life for its members is certainly to support a substantive ideal of a good human life. It is one in which everyone has sufficient means and developed capacity to take responsibility for their own lives and involves commitment to the range of practices described in Part I of this book. But if we put aside that obvious point, what these thinkers are supposing is that, if the state restricts itself to ensuring that everyone has an equal chance of achieving her autonomous choices, it will not be discriminating between the different choices of ideals its members make within the liberal paradigm. It will, therefore, exclude the pursuit of any particular ideal of the good life from its considerations and hence be anti-perfectionist.

Joseph Raz, whose own perfectionist theory of liberalism I will be discussing in the next section, criticizes this view on the grounds that some conceptions of the good life are worthless or even demeaning, and the state should not defend or promote people's opportunities to pursue such values. He accepts that there exists a plurality of valuable conceptions of the good and believes that the state has a duty to promote the availability of such ideals. While not disagreeing with Raz on the plurality of desirable values and on the state's duty to ensure that there are significant and valuable choices for its members to make, nevertheless I believe that qua liberal state it must defend its members' right to make bad choices. It is, rather, qua state that the state's concern with substantive values and ideals arises. As a state it is necessarily concerned with the community's economic prosperity, with the advancement and transmission of knowledge, the pursuit of the arts and excellence in sport. The state's support for these activities makes possible the autonomous choice by its members of the valuable ideals that are contained in them. The pursuit of liberal values must be understood in the context of a liberal state being first and foremost a state with the natural ends of the state as such.

THE PERFECTIONIST LIBERALISM OF JOSEPH RAZ (1939–)

The basic structure of Raz's argument for liberalism is simple and clear: the negative freedom mandated by liberalism is justified in order to protect the good of personal autonomy. By personal autonomy Raz means autonomy in respect of the control of our personal lives. It is not moral autonomy and does not include participation in the determination of the collective life of one's society. It involves rather the choice of ends and means for the conduct of one's personal life. But as this requires judgement of what ends are valuable for individuals to pursue in the organization of their personal life, it must allow for a critical evaluation of the values on offer in their society. The autonomous person, Raz says, "is a part author of his own life . . . fashioning it through successive decisions" throughout his life.[13] He is only a part author because he is also a product of his society and genetic inheritance. Within those constraints, the laws protecting and promoting liberal negative freedom allow him, and indeed more or less require him, to take a succession of decisions determining how his life will go.

Why does Raz think that autonomy is a good? He does not think that it is a good in itself because he believes that autonomously choosing worthless or evil outcomes does not add a little bit of goodness to the otherwise bad outcomes. For autonomy to be good for a person, she must have an adequate range of valuable options to choose between and she must choose some worthwhile end.[14] So autonomy would seem to be at best a necessary but not sufficient part of a good life. A good life for Raz is one which is rich in valuable activities and achievements. Yet, according to Raz, such a life may not be autonomously chosen. What, then, is the point of autonomy? It would not seem to be even a necessary condition of a good life. If the valuable activities are autonomously chosen, does this make the life better? But how can it be better if autonomy does not by itself add some value? It looks as though, for Raz, autonomy becomes a value when it forms the way through which valuable lives are arrived at. So, it is of value when exercised in the achievement of valuable activities but of no value when not attached to the attainment of good ends. However, if, as Raz believes, it is possible to organize society in such a way that its members can enjoy a good human life rich in valuable activities without autonomy, then why bother with autonomy?

One answer that Raz gives is that, if one lives in a society that requires autonomy in order to live a successful life within it and promotes the ideal of an autonomous life, then one has no choice but to try to develop one's own autonomous capacities.[15] Obviously, the individual by herself would have no choice in those circumstances whether or not to embrace an autonomous life. Such a life would be thrust upon her. But it would not follow that, collectively, they could not remove the autonomy- promoting features of their society. They could abolish the laws protecting negative freedom and return to the authoritarian structures of illiberal societies. Furthermore, it does not show that a society organized around personal autonomy is better than one in which there is very little scope for its exercise. At this point, Raz is inclined to say that an autonomy-based society is more appropriate to the conditions of modern life than one without autonomy. He has in mind the complexity and rapid economic change that characterizes that life.[16] Yet, this does not seem to be the right kind of claim for Raz to make. Autonomy becomes of instrumental value for a successful economy, not for lives rich in valuable activities.

One important thesis which Raz holds that may affect his answer to the questions I am pressing on him is his anti-individualistic communitarianism.[17] According to this view, an individual can only form a conception of a valuable end to pursue in his life on the basis of social forms and activities already present in his society. He may succeed in innovating in respect of these forms, but apparently, he cannot invent a new form of valuable activity. Thus, he holds that a person cannot choose to pursue a career as an architect if there is in his society no architectural profession; neither can a person choose to become a birdwatcher if this is not already an established activity. These seem to me to be misleading claims, but their relevance to his views on autonomy would be that in a society committed to promoting autonomous personal lives in its members, the members cannot but adopt, or at most innovate on the basis of, this form of life. So, one thing they would appear not to be able to do is demolish the forms of autonomous life in their society. For them, autonomy would be a necessary value. Yet, such demolition work is clearly very possible and has been done to different degrees in various modern societies such as Germany, Italy, Russia which extinguished some liberal forms for fascist or communist models of collective life.

In any case, to claim that autonomy is a good for societies that have developed autonomy-based ways of living but not otherwise good is not a theory of liberalism as I have been envisaging it. It does not give us reasons for preferring an autonomy-based way of life to the converse. The way to avoid this problem is to treat autonomy as the development of capacities that are the essential human capacities. If they are not present at all, the life is not a human one. The greater their development in harmony with our other capacities, the more fully human life will be and as such better for humans. These capacities can be used in pursuit of bad ends. This is merely to recognize that a distinctively human life may be a bad one.

There is another problem in Raz's account of liberalism. He has no theory of equality. He assumes that the rights mandated by the value of personal autonomy will be enjoyed by all equally. But he actually rejects equality as a relevant principle. He recognizes only a humanistic principle that human life is of intrinsic importance and rejects Dworkin's claim that this entails a strong egalitarian organization of society.[18]

You would think then that in order to support a liberal society based on equal rights of the members to the protection and promotion of their personal autonomy, you would need to show that everyone's life was of sufficient intrinsic importance to warrant their entitlement to such equal rights.

The reason why one might doubt that Raz can justify an egalitarian stance on rights to autonomy, is that he accepts that autonomy is a matter of degree and that human lives are better or worse according to the amount of goodness to be found in them. So if some people have a greater capacity than others for the exercise of personal autonomy and can achieve a higher level of goodness in their lives, should their society not discriminate in their favour?

Finally, there is the matter of Raz's perfectionism. His theory is grounded in an appeal to the value of personal autonomy. So it is not neutral between different conceptions of the good; neither does it exclude ideals from political consideration. It is squarely built on a conception of the good and promotes the ideal of a personally autonomous life. Because he believes that autonomy is no good unless exercised in pursuit of valuable ends, he holds the state to be under a duty to ensure that an adequate range of valuable options exists for people to choose between and to eliminate bad or worthless options. This would possibly involve quite a high degree of paternalism and seems doubtfully justifiable in a liberal regime. Of course, a liberal regime must exclude choices that involve the violation of the liberal rights of others and must aim to ensure a level playing field in economic and social transactions. But these restrictions are not paternalistically inspired by the aim of getting people to live better lives but by a concern for freedom and equality. I have also acknowledged that a state qua state rather than qua liberal state has interests in promoting its flourishing that should lead it to engage in activities that would not be justified by its liberal character alone. Finally, qua liberal, the state has a fundamental interest in providing an education to its members that would enable them to operate successfully within its liberal forms, including the ability to understand the reasons for living liberally. Raz believes that a state has authority over its subjects only insofar as it enables them to act better for the reasons for action that they already have independently of the state.[19] Since what they have most reason to do is to live a valuable life, the state may act to promote this end paternalistically. I would say that from a liberal point of view what the members have most reason to do is to take responsibility for their lives, and while the liberal state must promote this end and while it must provide an education for its members that enables them to judge between valuable and worthless ends, it should not otherwise be in the business of directing them to living the good life. In that sense, I am anti-perfectionist in respect of my liberalism also.

NOTES TOWARDS A BETTER THEORY OF LIBERALISM

In any such construction we must begin with the Rawlsian setting for the enquiry: a collection of persons already possessing a "we" identity as members of an independent political society re-evaluating together the terms of their political association. However, we can dispense with the mechanism of the veil of ignorance and suppose only that they are reasonable people seeking agreement on common rules and institutions that will be binding on all. This idea of political association involves the view that it is an arrangement whereby a collection of individuals commit themselves to pursue their fundamental interests through the acceptance of a "we" identity which is to be expressed in common rules and institutions that regulate the members' interactions. This formula is not itself an expression of a secular liberal understanding of political association. It leaves open how we are to understand people's fundamental interests. Thus, it is perfectly compatible with the endorsement of regimes based on elite knowledge of such interests interpreted in theological, economic or even racial terms and hence with the Islamic State of Iran or the Communist State of China or even the Nazi State of Germany. All such regimes must claim that elite rule is justified in terms of defending and promoting the fundamental interests of the members. (Of course, racist regimes define membership in terms of race so that only the interests of members of the race count.)

Why should we not start with the idea of individuals as independents in a state of nature understood as a morally free zone in the manner of Hobbes or as governed by a law of nature as in the libertarian theories of Locke and Nozick? Because, in the first place, as we have seen, you cannot gain an adequate theory of the state out of such premises, and, in the second place, the premise is fundamentally in conflict with the understanding of human nature as essentially social. On the latter view, the human capacities of rationality, autonomy and individuality presuppose this sociality as the necessary context in which they arise in us. Hence, the state of nature hypothesis abolishes at a stroke the background from which we emerge as reasoning and autonomous beings.

What I have earlier called the formula is, however, not compatible with totalizing conceptions of the good to be pursued through political association. Utilitarian maximization is a classic example of such a totalizing conception: what is right or wrong is determined by what does or does not maximize the total amount of utility summed over all persons or all sentient beings. The ethical objection to this is that it permits sacrificing some people's interests for the sake of larger gains accruing to others. This is objectionable, not because it does not count the interests of the sacrificed person but because it treats all persons as merely means for maximizing a total. They are not ends in themselves where this requires that their fundamental interests as a person cannot be overridden for the sake of increasing a larger total of something. Other totalizing conceptions involve treating the particular individual as merely a means to the realization of some goal such as a higher state of civilization, the advancement of the human race through its superior types, the actualization of rational freedom in the state or under communism. From these perspectives, it is not important whether any particular individual's fundamental interests are respected or not since such persons are only valuable as means to the promotion of the goal.

Treating all such totalizing views as unethical is to commit to a view of the ethical as requiring the recognition of each person as an end in herself, where this means that the terms of political association must aim at protecting and promoting the fundamental interests of each associate. It could be said that the acceptance of such a view of the ethical would not stop regimes adopting a totalizing conception of their goal. But the advocates of such a regime would have to acknowledge explicitly in the Rawlsian original position that they intended to treat everybody as a means to the proposed goal. I do not see how reasonable people concerned with the pursuit of their fundamental interests could accept such a ground for the terms of their political association. It is possible for people to see themselves in this way. But it is a kind of delirium in which one finds one's purpose and power in dedication to some abstract entity such as God, humanity, the race, the party and so on. If they grasp that the collectivity to which they are to subject themselves is just themselves committed to pursuing their fundamental interests together through binding common rules and institutions, they would not agree to any scheme that did not treat them as ends. Furthermore, they have to realize that in dedicating themselves to these abstract entities, they are in effect committing themselves to promote the interests of those who claim to speak for them – the priests, imams, party leaders and so on. The antidotes to this disease are the rule of law and democratic accountability and above all the ethical idea of individuals as ends in themselves.

Yet, I have acknowledged that understanding the ethical in the above way does not already give us the basis for a liberal theory or commit us to a human rights view of political order. It is compatible with what I have called Platonism. We need a theory that tells us why Platonism should be rejected and liberalism adopted. Remember, however, that the "we" here are the members of an existing political society committed to their unity under common rules trying to decide what set of proposals would be the best.

First of all, this liberal theory will contain a theory of freedom which tells us why we should value leaving people free to decide for themselves what to believe and how to live in the major spheres of life. We must reject the proposal that we should see each other as having a natural right to freedom as the basis of these rights for the reasons given earlier. The only plausible alternative is that we value autonomy as the basis of our freedom rights. Even the maximizing utilitarians have to appeal to a version of autonomy as one of the secondary values supporting a liberal organization of society. Since the totalizing aim unqualified by ethical considerations has been ruled out, the theory of freedom based on the value of autonomy must explain its worth in terms of its character as the expression of the fundamental human quality through which we exercise self-control in our thoughts and actions. This conception of the distinctive human powers is perfectly compatible with a belief in an omnipotent and benevolent deity, provided one sees him as creating us with these powers immediately or through a process of evolution, and does not suppose that he, absurdly, contradicts himself by requiring us to follow, uncritically, for eternity the thoughts and sayings of someone who lived over 1,000 years ago.

The theory of freedom tells us that we should value freedom for the sake of autonomy, but it does not tell us how this freedom should be distributed. To get to the standard liberal view that what is required is an equal freedom, we need a theory of equality. The simplest theory here is the view I have called liberal egalitarianism: each person is of inherent and absolute worth and hence of equal worth. This view has several severe defects. It first of all identifies worth independently of membership of the community. So, everyone in the world has the same worth as the members of one's community. This is not a proper basis for the special relation between members of a political association that we are investigating. Second, absolute worth is not the same as equal worth in the sense required for a system of mutually limiting equal rights that liberalism is. A collection of beings possessing absolute worth would have no interest in limiting that worth to fit in with a scheme of equal rights. Finally, the individual in her particularity as this person with her particular attributes cannot be considered to be of absolute worth. Were that to be the case, the most loathsome and evil person would have to be held to be of absolute worth. It only begins to make sense to attribute absolute worth to a person insofar as we see her, in her particularity, as a bearer of some transcendent value such as being created in the image of God or, as it turns out in Kant's theory, the bearer of pure rational will. But such a move allows you to kill off the particular individual if she is not fulfilling her designated role as the means through which transcendent worth is given actuality.

So, we need, first of all, an account of the worth present in the very idea of an ethical association – the commitment to protect and promote the fundamental interests of each member. I have already given such an account in my earlier remarks about the nature of ethical association. The members of the association are committed to recognizing each other as ends and thus as entitled to have their fundamental interests protected in any proposed terms. But, then, we come back, second, to the need to give reasons for distributing liberal rights equally to all. We cannot claim that such an equal distribution is mandated by the fact that all possess the capacity for autonomy to an equal degree. This is manifestly false. The alternative is to claim that all possess the capacity to a sufficient degree to pass a threshold level of capacity that entitles them to the rights. Although inequalities beyond the threshold will exist, they will be deemed irrelevant to the distribution of rights. However, the theory will have to show why the inequalities beyond the threshold are irrelevant. The view I take, at this point, is that possessing the threshold capacity ensures that each person's fundamental interest can be satisfied only if she enjoys the full liberal rights. A society in which each person enjoys the full liberal rights will be one in which there exists an equality of such rights.

Furthermore, an equal distribution would, all things considered, be a better arrangement than any alternative. It would be better because, first, the threshold level capacity to take responsibility for one's life will ensure that leaving people free to run their own lives will produce better results than subjecting some number of them to patronizing control by an elite. While some people will no doubt make a mess of their lives, there will be a higher level of attainment in the liberal regime of the fundamental human value of autonomy than in less free illiberal regimes. Second, without the right of an elite to impose its view of what people should believe and how they should live, there will be much less oppression, stress and potentially violent conflict in the liberal regime than in illiberal ones. Of course, it has to be recognized that the liberal regime gives an elite – the liberal elite – the right and duty to make and enforce laws that protect the liberal rights and to promote the liberal ideas through the ideological institutions of the society. Yet, that elite has no right to forbid people to think illiberal thoughts or to organize themselves in illiberal forms of life provided they respect the Brandenburg principle, and in a liberal-democracy the elite will be subject to the rule of law and democratic accountability. In this sense, liberalism while enforcing its form of life to some degree on everyone, nevertheless is a vastly less oppressive and vastly freer society than the standard alternatives. While this argument involves an appeal to the good consequences of adopting a liberal regime, it is an appeal made within the constraints set by the principles of ethical association which demand the recognition of each associate and her fundamental interest as an end for all the others.

Insofar as the argument for an equal distribution of freedom rights rests crucially on the attainment of a threshold level of capacity for autonomy and on the irrelevance of inequalities in the capacity beyond the threshold, the claims of any form of egalitarian liberalism must be abandoned. What level of resources a member of a liberal society would be entitled to claim for his support and development would be whatever is enough to enable him to develop his powers to reach and sustain the threshold level of autonomy. While that idea leaves much open for debate regarding what the actual level of entitlement would be, at least the general idea of sufficientism would be a great advance on the absences of communal spirit and solidaristic welfare in libertarianism and the hostility to superiority and excellence in egalitarianism.

This theory would, thus, have shown how the ethical status of individuals as ends can be grounded in the very idea of members of an independent political society committed to interacting on the basis of common rules and institutions. It will have shown why we should be interested in recognizing and protecting freedom rights and why these rights should be distributed equally. An aspect of the latter argument will be an appeal to the level of well-being attainable in well-ordered liberal states as compared with illiberal ones. The theory will have justified an equal freedom in the context of a commitment to the value of community and a claim about the level of well-being in liberal societies.

One obvious defect in this sketch of a better liberal theory than those discussed in Part III is that the theory applies only to an independent political society and does not mention its possible application to international society or the world. I have in fact discussed in Part II the issues that arise for liberal states in a multi-state world where some powerful states are illiberal and even hostile to liberalism, and I have nothing new to add to that discussion. I will reiterate, nevertheless, the absolute necessity of the maintenance, for the foreseeable future, of viable independent political societies having the form of nation-states for international society. What order that anarchical society possesses depends on the order provided by the various states. They provide the order that exists within their own territories and make it possible for foreigners to benefit from it. But for the latter to happen, the states must create and uphold an international society through agreements regarding a multiplicity of international rules and institutions, and they must regulate their own state to state interactions bearing on the deployment and use of their vast military forces. How this society can be managed when internally the main actors follow different rules and endorse different values, I have discussed in the appropriate section in the text. But it is certain that if every state insists on putting its interests first in such an arena, there will be no order and little future.

FURTHER READING

Rawls (1993, 1999); Dworkin (1977, 2000, 2011); Raz (1986).
On Rawls, Dworkin and Raz, read Kymlicka (1990) and Mulhall and Swift (1996).
On Rawls, see Kukathas and Pettit (1990).
On Dworkin, see Macleod (1998). On Raz, see Meyer (2003).

NOTES

1 Rawls (1999, pp.10–14).
2 Ibid., pp.15–18.
3 Ibid., p.54.
4 Rawls (1980).
5 Ibid., p.266.
6 Ibid., p.107. The actual list on p.107 differs somewhat from the one I describe. Mine omits egoistic conceptions of justice as being fairly pointless and treats perfectionism as one of the main alternatives rather than as a subset of teleological principles.
7 Rawls (1993, p.13).
8 Dworkin (1977, pp.272–3).
9 Dworkin (1983).
10 Dworkin (1981).
11 Dworkin (2000, pp.1, 6).
12 Dworkin (2011, p.327).
13 Raz (1986, p.369).

14 Ibid., p.381.
15 Ibid., p.391.
16 Ibid., pp.369–70.
17 Ibid., pp.307–11.
18 Ibid., Chap. 9, passim.
19 Ibid., p.53.

REFERENCES

Anderson, E. (1999) "What is the Point of Equality?" *Ethics* 109/2 pp.287–337.
Appiah, K.A. (2005) *The Ethics of Identity* (Princeton, NJ: Princeton University Press).
Aristotle (1921) *Politics*, tr. B. Jowett (Oxford, UK: Clarendon Press).
Baggini, J. (2015) *Freedom Regained* (London: Granta Books).
Barendt, E. (2007) *Freedom of Speech* (Oxford, UK: Oxford University Press).
Barry, B. and Goodin, R. (eds.) (1992) *Free Movement: Ethical Issues in the Transnational Migration of People and Money* (Abingdon, UK: Routledge).
Bentham, J. (1982) *An Introduction to the Principles of Morals and Legislation*, eds. Burns, J. and Hart, H. (London: Athlone Press).
Berger, R. (1997) *Government by Judiciary: The Transformation of the Fourteenth Amendment* (Indianapolis, IN: Liberty Fund).
Berlin, I. (1969) *Four Essays on Liberty* (Oxford, UK: Oxford University Press).
———. (1978) *Concepts and Categories: Philosophical Essays, Vol 2* (London: Hogarth Press).
Betts, A. and Collier, P. (2017) *Refuge: Transforming a Broken Refugee System* (New York: Penguin Random House).
Bingham, T. (2011) *The Rule of Law* (London: Penguin Books).
Boucher, D. and Kelly, P. (2003) *Political Thinkers from Socrates to the Present* (Oxford, UK: Oxford University Press).
Bull, H. (1977) *The Anarchical Society* (London: Macmillan).
Butler, J. (1990) *Gender Trouble* (Abingdon, UK: Routledge).

Charvet, J. (1982) *Feminism* (London: J.M. Dent).

———. (2013) *The Nature and Limits of Human Equality* (London: Palgrave Macmillan).

Charvet, J. and Kaczynska-Nay, E. (2008) *The Liberal Project and Human Rights* (Cambridge, UK: Cambridge University Press).

Connolly, W. (2005) *Pluralism* (Durham, NC: Duke University Press).

Crisp, R. (2013) "Well-Being" in Zalta, E.N. (ed.) *The Stanford Encyclopedia of Philosophy*.

Dawisha, K. (2014) *Putin's Kleptocracy: Who Owns Russia?* (New York: Simon and Schuster).

Dixon, M. (2000) *Textbook on International Law* (London: Blackstone Press).

Donnelly, J. (2000) *Realism and International Relations* (Cambridge, UK: Cambridge University Press).

Dworkin, G. (1990) *The Theory and Practice of Autonomy* (Cambridge, UK: Cambridge University Press).

Dworkin, R. (1977) *Taking Rights Seriously* (London: Duckworth).

———. (1981) "What is Equality?" *Philosophy and Public Affairs* 10/3,4 pp.185–246 and 283–345.

———. (2000) *Sovereign Virtue* (Cambridge, MA: Harvard University Press).

———. (2011) *Justice for Hedgehogs* (Cambridge, MA: Harvard University Press).

Fawcett, E. (2014) *Liberalism: The Life of an Idea* (Princeton, NJ: Princeton University Press).

Fenby, J. (2012) *Tiger Head, Snake Tail. China Today, How it Got There, and Where it is Heading* (New York: Simon and Schuster).

Flikschuh, K. (2000) *Kant and Modern Political Philosophy* (Cambridge, UK: Cambridge University Press).

Frankfurt, H. (1987) "Equality as a Moral Ideal" *Ethics* 98 pp.21–43.

Freeden, M. (1978) *The New Liberalism: An Ideology of Social Reform* (Oxford, UK: Oxford University Press).

———. (2015) *Liberalism: A Very Short Introduction* (Oxford, UK: Oxford University Press).

Friedan, B. (1965) *The Feminine Mystique* (London: Penguin Books).

Garton Ash, T. (2016) *Free Speech* (London: Atlantic Books).

Gessen, M. (2012) *The Man Without a Face: The Unlikely Rise of Vladimir Putin* (New York: Penguin Random House).

Gilligan, C. (1983) *In a Different Voice: Psychological Theory and Women's Development* (Cambridge, MA: Harvard University Press).

Gould, J. (2005) *Speak No Evil: The Triumph of Hate Speech Regulation* (Chicago, IL: Chicago University Press).

Gray, J. (2015) *The Soul of the Marionette* (New York: Penguin Random House).

Greenwald, G. (2014) *No Place to Hide: Edward Snowden, the NSA and the Surveillance State* (London: Hamish Hamilton).

Griffin, J. (1986) *Well-Being: Its Meaning, Measurement and Moral Importance* (Oxford, UK: Clarendon Press).

Hampsher-Monk, I. (1992) *A History of Modern Political Thought* (Oxford, UK: Blackwell).

Harding, L. (2014) *The Snowden Files: The Inside Story of the World's Most Wanted Man* (New York: Vintage Books).

Hare, R. (1981) *Moral Thinking* (Oxford, UK: Clarendon Press).

Haworth, A. (2015) *Free Speech* (London: Hodder and Stoughton).

Held, D. (1995) *Democracy and Global Order* (Cambridge, UK: Polity Press).

Hill, T. (1992) *Dignity and Practical Reason* (Ithaca, NY: Cornell University Press).

Hobhouse, L.T. (1964 [1911]) *Liberalism* (New York: Oxford University Press).

Honore, A.M. (1961) "Ownership", in Guest, A.M. (ed.) *Oxford Essays in Jurisprudence* (Oxford, UK: Oxford University Press).

Jarman, N. (1997) *Material Conflicts: Parades and Visual Displays in Northern Ireland* (Oxford, UK: Oxford University Press).

Jones, P. (2016) "Group Rights" in Zalta, E.N. (ed.) *The Stanford Encyclopedia of Philosophy* (Summer 2016 Edition).

Kant, I. (1965) *The Metaphysical Elements of Justice*, tr. J. Ladd (New York: The Liberal Arts Press)

———. (1993) *Grounding for the Metaphysics of Morals*, tr. J. Ellington (Indianapolis, IN: Hackett Publishing Co.).

Kara, S. (2017) *Modern Slavery: A Global Perspective* (New York: Columbia University Press).

Krasner, S. (1999) *Sovereignty: Organized Hypocrisy* (Princeton, NJ: Princeton University Press).

Kukathas, C. and Pettit, P. (1990) *Rawls: A Theory of Justice and its Critics* (Cambridge, UK: Polity Press).

Kymlicka, W. (1990) *Contemporary Political Philosophy: an Introduction* (Oxford, UK: Oxford University Press).

Lacey, N. (2004) "Feminist Legal Theory and the Rights of Women" in Knop, K. (ed.) *Gender and Human Rights* (Oxford, UK: Oxford University Press).

La Rochefoucauld (1981) *Maxims*, tr. L. Tancock (London: Penguin Classics).

Lloyd Thomas, D. (1979) "Equality Within the Limits of Reason" *Mind* 88/352 pp.538–53.

———. (1995) *Locke on Government* (Abingdon, UK: Routledge).

Locke, J. (1964) *Two Treatises of Government*, ed. P. Laslett (Cambridge, UK: Cambridge University Press).

Lukanoff, G. (2012) *Unlearning Liberty: Campus Censorship and the End of American Debate* (New York: Encounter Books).

Lyons, D. (1965) *The Forms and Limits of Utilitarianism* (Oxford, UK: Clarendon Press).

MacIntyre, A. (1981) *After Virtue* (London: Duckworth).

Macleod, C. (1998) *Liberalism, Justice and Markets: A Critique of Liberal Equality* (Oxford, UK: Oxford University Press).

Marx, K. (1990) *Capital Vol I* (London: Penguin Books).

Mason, A. (ed.) (1998) *Ideals of Equality* (Oxford, UK: Blackwell).

McWilliams, P. (1993) *Ain't Nobody's Business if you Do: The Absurdity of Consensual Crimes in a Free Society* (London: Prelude Press).

Mead, D. (2010) *The New Law of Peaceful Protest: Rights and Regulations in the 'Human Rights Act Era* (Oxford, UK: Hart Publishing Co.).

Merquior, J. (1991) *Liberalism, Old and New* (Cambridge, UK: Cambridge University Press).

Meyer, L. (ed.) (2003) *Rights, Culture and the Law: Themes from the Legal and Political Philosophy of Joseph Raz* (Oxford, UK: Oxford University Press).

Mill, J.S. (2015) *On Liberty, Utilitarianism and Other Essays*, eds. Philp, M. and Rosen, F. (Oxford, UK: Oxford University Press).

Miller, D. (ed.) (1991) *Liberty* (Oxford, UK: Oxford University Press).

———. (1998) "Justice and Equality" in Mason, A. (ed.) *Ideals of Equality* (Oxford, UK: Blackwell).

———. (2007) *National Responsibility and Global Justice* (Oxford, UK: Oxford University Press).

Moore, M. (2001) *The Ethics of Nationalism* (Oxford, UK: Oxford University Press).

Mulhall, S. and Swift, A. (1996) *Liberals and Communitarians* Second Edition (Oxford, UK: Blackwell).

Nozick, R. (1974) *Anarchy, State and Utopia* (Oxford, UK: Blackwell).

Parekh, B. (ed.) (1972) *Bentham's Political Thought* (London: Croom Helm).

Pecoud, A. (ed.) (2010) *Migration without Borders: Essays on the Free Movement of People* (New York: Berghahn Books).

Rawls, J. (1980) "Kantian Constructivism in Moral Theory" *Journal of Philosophy* 77/9, pp.515–72.

———. (1993) *Political Liberalism* (New York: Columbia University Press).

———. (1999) *A Theory Of Justice* Revised Edition (Oxford, UK: Oxford University Press).

Raz, J. (1986) *The Morality of Freedom* (Oxford, UK: Clarendon Press).

Rousseau, J.-J. (1964) *The Social Contract*, tr. M. Cranston (London: Penguin Books).

———. (1968) *The Discourse on the Origins of Inequality*, trs. R. and J. Masters (London: St Martin's Press).

Ruggiero, G. de (1927) *The History of European Liberalism*, tr. R. Collingwood (Oxford, UK: Oxford University Press).

Sandel, M. (1982) *Liberalism and the Limits of Justice* (Cambridge, UK: Cambridge University Press).

Smart, J. and Williams, B. (1973) *Utilitarianism: For and Against* (Cambridge, UK: Cambridge University Press).

Smith, A. (2001) *National Identity* (London: Penguin Books).

Sneddon, A. (2013) *Autonomy* (London: Bloomsbury Publishing).

Sumner, L. (1996) *Welfare, Happiness and Ethics* (Oxford, UK: Oxford University Press).

Swift, A. (2001) *Political Philosophy: A Beginner's Guide for Students and Politicians* (Cambridge, UK: Polity Press).

Tamanaha, B. (2004) *On the Rule of Law* (Cambridge, UK: Cambridge University Press).

Taylor, C. (1985) *Philosophical Papers, vols 1&2* (Cambridge, UK: Cambridge University Press).

_____. (1990) *Sources of the Self* (Cambridge, UK: Cambridge University Press).

Temkin, L. (1993) *Inequality* (Oxford, UK: Oxford University Press).

United Nations (1996) *Basic Human Rights Instruments* (Geneva: Office of the High Commissioner for Human Rights).

Vallentyne, P. (2002) "Libertarianism" in Zalta, E.N. (ed.) *The Stanford Encyclopedia of Philosophy* (Fall 2002 Edition).

Vincent, N. (2012) *Magna Carta: A Very Short Introduction* (Oxford, UK: Oxford University Press).

Wacks, R. (2010) *Privacy: A Very Short Introduction* (Oxford, UK: Oxford University Press).

Wall, S. (ed.) (2015) *Liberalism* (Cambridge, UK: Cambridge University Press).

Walzer, M. (1983) *Spheres of Justice* (Cambridge, UK: Cambridge University Press).

_____. (1987) *Interpretation and Social Criticism* (Cambridge, MA: Harvard University Press).

_____. (1994) *Thick and Thin: Moral Argument at Home and Abroad* (Notre Dame, IN: Notre Dame University Press).

Warburton, N. (2009) *Free Speech: A Very Short Introduction* (Oxford, UK: Oxford University Press).

Watson, A. (1972) *The Evolution of International Society* (Abingdon, UK: Routledge).

Weedon, C. (1999) *Feminism, Theory and the Politics of Difference* (Oxford, UK: Blackwell).

Weeks, J. (1981) *Sex, Politics and Society: the Regulation of Sexuality since 1800* (London: Longman Publishing Group).

Weldon, T. (1953) *The Vocabulary of Politics* (London: Penguin Books).

White, S. (2007) *Equality* (Cambridge, UK: Polity Press).

Wilkinson, R. and Pickett, K. (2009) *The Spirit Level: Why Equality is Better for Everyone* (London: Penguin Books).

Wolff, J. (1991) *Robert Nozick: Property, Justice and the Minimal State* (Palo Alto, CA: Stanford University Press).

———. (1998) "Fairness, Respect and the Egalitarian Ethos" *Philosophy and Public Affairs* 27/2 pp.97–122.

Wolin, S. (2017) *Democracy Incorporated: Managed Democracy and the Specter of Inverted Totalitarianism* Second Edition (Princeton, NJ: Princeton University Press).

Wood, A. (1999) *Kant's Ethical Thought* (Cambridge, UK: Cambridge University Press).

Young, I.M. (1990) *Justice and the Politics of Difference* (Princeton, NJ: Princeton University Press).

Young, M. (1958) *The Rise of the Meritocracy* (London: Penguin Books).

Young, R. (2017) *Personal Autonomy: Beyond Negative and Positive Liberty* (Abingdon, UK: Routledge).

INDEX

anti-discrimination laws 45–6
Aristotle, 88–9
autonomy: essential human capacity 76–7, 193, 198; and free will 70–1; general possession of sufficient degree of 132; matter of degree 69–70, 72, 77, 83–4, 194, 199; nature of 68–75; and rational agency 69, 70, 126, 128–9; and reflective evaluation 72, 73, 133; and responsibility 71, 72, 73, 75, 81, 88, 199; threshold levels of 77, 84, 185, 199; two levels of 72–3, 128–30, 132, 133, 150; value of 76–7; *see also* freedom: and worth of options

Bentham, J. 138, 140, 153; liberalism of 156–9
Berlin, Sir Isaiah 65, 68
Brandenburg rule 25–6, 39, 131, 199

Campbell, N., invasion of privacy 19
China 5, 11, 22, 23–5, 38, 112, 120, 123n3, 195

civil society 35; international 118, 120, 122, 123
Connolly, W. 96–9
communitarianism 99–101
community: ethical nature of 101, 104, 198, 199; and independent political society xv, 43, 62–3, 110–12: and moral equality of members 84; unreflective type of 133–4
compulsory insurance schemes 47–8
consumer protection laws 44–5

democracy: illiberal or managed 11–12, 83, 112, 131; liberal 82, 99, 112, 130–1; and rule of law 12–13; vulnerability of 34–5, 130–1
Dworkin, R. 85, 138, 182, 184–91, 194

egalitarianism: luck 85, 188–9; *see also* liberal egalitarianism
equality: concept of 79–80; as distributive principle 79; moral 84; of outcome or resources 85, 87;

as social and political ideal 80; of status xv, 43, 79–83, 87; as value in itself 86
European Convention of Human Rights 19
European Court of Justice 20
European Union 38, 39, 113, 122

family: nature of 59, 105
feminism: difference 58, 90–1; and equality 88–94; liberal 57, 88–9; post-modern 92
free association: difference between criminal and ideological laws 33–4
freedom: and existence of options 66, 75–6; and law 68; and moral constraints 58–9; negative and positive 65, 68, 75; triadic conception of 65, 68; value of 76; and worth of options 67, 74, 87, 151
free speech: divergence between liberal and illiberal regimes on 22–25; and norms of civility 29–30; standard constraints on 18–22

Google 19–20
groups: rights of 103–6

Hare, R.M. 154
hate speech laws 23; UK laws on 26; reasons for and against 26–7
Hitler, A. 13, 14
Hobbes, T. 138, 196

identity: cultural 86–7; and egalitarianism 101–3; and feminism 89–91; and multi-culturalism 96–103; national 103, 112–16, 133; "we" 133, 150, 151, 195, 197; *see also* groups: rights of
individuals: absolute worth of 84, 198; *see also* Kant: absolute worth of persons
International Covenant on Civil and Political Rights 23, 36, 101

international society 116–23, 200–1; liberal states' strategies in 120–3; "liberal" view of 119–20; realist view of 117–20
Islamic states illiberalism: constraints on free speech 24; constraints on sexual freedom 56; constraints on women 37

Kant, I. 138, 140; and absolute worth of persons 167, 169–71, 174; and negative freedom 171–2; and totalizing ethical thinking 174

labour protection laws 43–4, 81
Lee Kuan Yew 13, 14
liberalism: and belief in God 134–6, 144, 198; and economic inequality 50, 80, 87–8; as matter of degree 4–6; and property rights 51–3
liberal egalitarianism xiv, 61–2, 80, 83–8; critique of 198–200
liberal practices: nature and origins of xii–xv, 4
liberal theories xv, 3, 137; historical development of 138–41
libertarianism xiv, 42, 44, 61–2, 75, 77, 85, 86; inadequacy of 148–51
Litvinenko, A. 31n9
Locke, J. 68, 82, 138, 144, 145, 146, 147, 196

Mill, J.S. 17, 25, 29, 56, 138, 153; and equality 163–4; and higher forms of life 161–3; and liberty 159–6
monopolies 45
multi-culturalism 28–9; egalitarian 102–3; identity-based 96–9; liberal 94–6

nation nature of 113–14
nation-states: importance of 113, 116, 200–1
NATO 122
natural rights theory 138–9; and the minimal state 146–8; and natural

liberty 143–4, 146; and property 144–5; and the state of nature 138, 145, 148, 196
Nozick, R. 77, 138, 144, 145, 147, 148, 150, 157, 190, 196

perfectionism and anti-perfectionism: Dworkin on 184, 190; Rawls on 178; Raz on 191, 194–5
platform: denial of 28–9
Platonism 77, 84, 178, 197
political correctness 6, 17, 29
political society (independent) xiii, xv, 24, 43, 62–3, 109, 112, 200, 201; as example of group rights 103–4; moral equality of members 84; as sphere of collective action 81–2; *see also* state: sovereign nature of; community
practice: nature of 1–4
public goods 46–7, 49
public opinion: moral coercion of 6, 17, 29
Putin, V. 11, 12, 14, 24, 31n9, 83, 131

Rawls, J. 85, 138, 140–1, 144, 176, 184, 186, 188, 189; on difference principle 177, 178–9, 181; as egalitarian liberal 177, 181; and libertarianism 178–9; on value neutrality 176, 181
Raz, J. 138, 191; on the good of autonomy 192–3; on negative freedom 191, 192; on equality 193–4
refugees 39–40, 103
Rousseau, J.J. 68, 80, 107n1, 136n1
rule of law: and corruption 10, 11, 12, 14; and government accountability in England 8–9; major abuses of 10–12; as opposed to rule of men/women 7–9; relation to liberal-democratic practices 12–13; in UN covenants and Declarations 10
Russia 11–12, 22, 24, 83, 122, 131

"safe places" 28
self-ownership 51
Singapore 13, 14, 42
Skripal, S. 31n9
slavery 42, 81
Snowden, E. 22, 31n7
socialism 51–2
soviet communism 11, 30, 53, 93, 99
state: sovereign nature of 35, 112, 140; and non-liberal goals of 43
structure of book explained xii–xiii
sufficientism 88, 128, 200

Temkin, L. 86
toleration xi, 97–9, 139
totalizing ethical thinking 154, 158, 174, 196, 197, 198
transgender people 93–4
Trump, D. 13, 123n3, 181

United Nations Organization 112, 120, 121, 123n4
universities: nature of 105
USA 5, 6, 14, 22, 23, 29, 36, 45, 46, 55, 112
US Supreme Court: bakers case 46; Brandenburg case 25; Brown vs. Board of Education 13; Hastings Christian legal society 36; and homosexuality 56
utilitarianism: basic structure of 153–4; and secondary principles 154–64; as totalizing doctrine 154, 158

well-being: and autonomy 128–30; and community 62, 63, 133–4; and material inequalities 126–7; and meritocracy 127; notion of 125

Taylor & Francis Group
an informa business

Taylor & Francis eBooks

www.taylorfrancis.com

A single destination for eBooks from Taylor & Francis with increased functionality and an improved user experience to meet the needs of our customers.

90,000+ eBooks of award-winning academic content in Humanities, Social Science, Science, Technology, Engineering, and Medical written by a global network of editors and authors.

TAYLOR & FRANCIS EBOOKS OFFERS:

- A streamlined experience for our library customers
- A single point of discovery for all of our eBook content
- Improved search and discovery of content at both book and chapter level

REQUEST A FREE TRIAL

support@taylorfrancis.com

Routledge
Taylor & Francis Group

CRC Press
Taylor & Francis Group